JavaScript Programming

for Beginners

How to Learn JavaScript in Less Than One Week. The Ultimate Step-by-Step Complete Course from Novice to Advance Programmer

William Brown

The information in the following pages is broadly considered a truthful and accurate account of facts and as such, any inattention, use, or misuse of the information in question by the reader will render any resulting actions solely under their purview. There are no scenarios in which the publisher or the original author of this work can be in any fashion deemed liable for any hardship or damages that may befall them after undertaking information described herein.

Additionally, the information in the following pages is intended only for informational purposes and should thus be thought of as universal. As befitting its nature, it is presented without assurance regarding its prolonged validity or interim quality. Trademarks that are mentioned are done without written consent and can in no way be considered an endorsement from the trademark holder.

Table of contents

Introduction

JavaScript is a scripting language that is interpreted and lightweight. It's made to help you create network-centric apps. It works in conjunction with Java and complements it. Since JavaScript is integrated with HTML, it's very simple to use. It is cross-platform and open source.

Benefits of JavaScript

JavaScript is a must-have skill for students & working professionals who want to become great software engineers, especially those who work in the Web Development field. A few of the main benefits of studying JavaScript:

- JavaScript is the most widely used programming language on the planet. It is an excellent option for programmers. When you study JavaScript, you will use various JavaScript-based applications like jQuery, Node.JS, and others to create amazing front-end and backend apps.

- JavaScript is everywhere; it's built into any modern web browser, so there's no need for a special configuration to learn it. Many browsers support JavaScript, including Chrome, Mozilla Firefox, Safari, and almost any other browser.

- JavaScript helps in building stunningly beautiful and lightning-fast websites. You should create a website with a console-like look and feel and have the greatest Graphical User Experience for your visitors.

- JavaScript is now used in game development, smartphone app production, and web app development. As a JavaScript programmer, this opens up a lot of possibilities for you.

- There is a lot of work development and a high salary for all those who know JavaScript due to high demand. You should look at various career boards and see what it's like to get JavaScript expertise in the job industry.

- The great thing regarding JavaScript is that there are already many frameworks & libraries available that can be included directly in the software development to minimize time to market.

- There may be a slew of compelling reasons to study JavaScript programming. But one thing is sure: to master every programming language, like JavaScript, all you have to do is write, code, code, and code some more before you're an expert.

Chapter No 1: JavaScript Basics

Every time a website does more than stay there and show static details for you to look at — showing timely content alerts, dynamic charts, animated 2D/3D images, scrolling video jukeboxes, and so on — you can guarantee that JavaScript is involved. It's the 3rd layer of a 3-layer cake of typical web technology, the first two of which are CSS and HTML.

CSS is a series of design guidelines that add styling to HTML text, such as changing background colors and fonts and arranging content in several columns.

HTML is the language used to format and add context to the web material, such as describing lines, headings, and data tables and embedding images and videos.

JavaScript is a scripting language for creating dynamically updated material, controlling multimedia, animating photos, and everything else. (Not anything, but it's incredible what a short JavaScript code will accomplish.)

1.1 Use of JavaScript

The JavaScript language's main client-side functionality include the following:

- Variables may be used to store valuable values. For example, in the above example, we ask for a new name and then store it in a variable named 'name'.

- Text manipulation operations (known as "strings" in programming). In the preceding case, we join the string "Player 1:" to the name variable to construct a full-text mark, such as "Player 1: Chris."

- As such activities arise on a web screen, coding is performed. In the previous case, we used a click event to detect when the button was pressed and then ran the code that updated the text mark.

- And a lot more!

However, the functionality installed on top of the client-side JavaScript language is much more exciting. Application Programming Interfaces (APIs) offer you extra superpowers that you can use in your JavaScript code.

APIs are pre-built sets of code that enable a developer to create programs that might otherwise be difficult or impossible to make. They are doing the same thing for programming that already prepared furniture kits to do for home construction. It's way simpler to take pre-cut panels and mount them together to create a bookshelf than it is to figure out the pattern yourself, find the suitable wood, cut all the pieces to the right shape and size, find the suitable screws, and then bring them all together to make a bookshelf.

They can be divided into two classes.

Browser APIs are integrated into your web browser and can expose data from your computer's surroundings or perform valuable complex tasks. Consider the following scenario:

The DOM (Document Object Model) API lets you modify HTML and CSS, including adding, deleting, and modifying HTML, as well as dynamically introducing different styles to your website. The DOM is in operation whenever you see a popup window appear on a website or new material shown (as we showed above in our easy demo).

The Geolocation API is used to get spatial data. It is how Google Maps locates and plots your position on a chart.

You may use the Canvas and WebGL APIs to make interactive 2D and 3D graphics. See Chrome Experiments and WebGL samples for examples of what people are doing using these web technologies.

HTMLMediaElement and WebRTC are audio and video APIs that enable you to do pretty cool stuff with multimedia, like play audio and video right on a web page or take video from your web camera and show it on someone else's screen.

Notice that all of the above demos would not fit in an older browser; while experimenting, it's best to run the code in a new browser like Firefox, Chrome, Edge, or Opera. As you move closer to shipping production code, you'll need to think about cross-browser checking in greater depth (i.e., actual code that real customers will use).

Third-party APIs aren't integrated into most browsers by design, so you'll have to find their code and documentation somewhere on the Internet. Consider the following scenario:

You may use the Twitter API to update the most recent tweets on your page, for example.

You will use the Google Maps API and the OpenStreetMap API to add personalized maps and other features to your website.

There's still a lot more to choose from! But don't get all worked up just yet. After learning JavaScript for 24 hours, you are not ready to create the next Google Maps, Facebook, or Instagram —

there are several fundamentals to learn first. That's why you're here, so let's get started!

1.2 JavaScript Presence on your page

You'll start looking through some code here, and while you're at it, you'll see what happens when you run JavaScript on your site.

Let's have a quick look at what occurs when you open a web page in a browser. When you open a web page in your window, your programming (HTML, CSS, and JavaScript) is executed inside an execution environment (the browser tab). It is similar to a factory that accepts raw materials (code) and produces a finished product (the web page).

The Document Object Model API is a popular way to use JavaScript to dynamically change HTML and CSS to update a user interface (as mentioned above). It's important to remember that the code in the web documents is usually loaded and executed to appear on the website. Errors will occur if the JavaScript loads and begins to operate until the HTML and CSS it affects have been loaded. In the segment on script loading techniques later in the part, you'll learn how to get around this.

Browser security

Every browser tab has its specific bucket for running code in (technically, these buckets are referred to as "execution environments"), which ensures that the code in each tab is typically executed entirely independently, and the code in one tab cannot explicitly affect the code in another tab — or on another website. It is a positive protection move because if it wasn't, pirates might start writing code to steal details from other websites and other malicious activities.

Note: There are specialized strategies for sending code and data across various websites/tabs in a secure manner that we will not discuss in this course.

Interpreted versus compiled code

In the sense of programming, you might hear the words translated and compiled. In translated languages, the code is executed from top to bottom, and the output of the execution is returned immediately. Before the browser runs the code, you don't have to convert it into a different format. The code is obtained in a programmer-friendly text format and is read immediately.

On the other hand, compiled languages are converted (compiled) into a different format before being run by a program. C/C++, for example, is converted into machine code and is then executed by the computer. The software is run in binary format, created from the source code of the original program.

JavaScript is an interpreted programming language that is lightweight. The JavaScript code is received in its original text type by the web browser, which then executes the document. To increase speed, many modern JavaScript interpreters use a technique known as just-in-time compilation, in which the JavaScript source code is converted into a quicker, binary format while the code is being used, allowing it to run as quickly as possible. The compilation is done at run time rather than ahead of time. JavaScript is also considered an interpreted language.

There are advantages to both types of language, but we won't discuss them right now.

Server-side versus client-side code

In the context of web development, you can often hear the words server-side and client-side coding. When a web page is opened, the client-side code is copied, and executed, and shown by the browser. We are specifically about client-side JavaScript in this module.

On the other hand, server-side JavaScript is executed on the server before being downloaded and viewed. PHP, Python, Ruby, ASP.NET, and JavaScript are examples of common server-side web languages. JavaScript may also be used as a server-side language, such as in the standard Node.js environment.

Dynamic versus static code

Dynamic refers to the capacity to change the view of a web page/app to reveal various objects under different contexts, create new material if required, and define both client-side JavaScript and server-side languages. Client-side JavaScript dynamically creates new content within the browser on the client, such as generating a new HTML table, loading it with data demanded from the server, and then showing the table in a web page displayed to the customer, while server-side JavaScript dynamically creates new content on the server, such as pulling data from a database. In both cases, the definition is somewhat different, but they are similar, and both methods (server-side and client-side) are commonly used together.

Static refers to a web page that does not have constantly updating functionality and displays similar content all the time

1.3 Running the JavaScript

JavaScript cannot function on its own because it is a scripting language. The server, in particular, is in charge of executing JavaScript code. When a user requests an HTML file that contains JavaScript, the script is submitted to the server, and the browser is responsible for executing it. The key benefit of JavaScript is that all modern web browsers support it. As a result, you won't have to think over whether the site visitors are using Internet Explorer, Google Chrome, Firefox, or another application. The use of JavaScript would be possible. JavaScript is also compatible with every operating system, like Windows, Linux, and Mac. As a result, JavaScript overcomes the significant drawbacks of VBScript (now deprecated) and is restricted to just Internet Explorer and Windows.

Tools You Need

First, you'll need a text editor and a browser to write the code and view the web pages you create. You may use any text editor you're comfortable with, such as Visual Studio Code, Notepad++, Atom, Sublime Text, or any other text editor. Any web browser, such as Firefox, Google Chrome, Microsoft Edge, and Internet Explorer, can be included.

A Simple JavaScript Program

If you choose to maintain the JavaScript code in the HTML document itself, use the <script> tags (<script> and </script>). It helps in the separation of the JavaScript project from the majority of the code in your window. There are some other client-side scripting languages (VBScript), specifying the scripting language is strongly suggested.

Note

Brendan Eich created JavaScript, a client-side scripting language.

JavaScript is compatible with nearly all operating systems and web browsers.

To write JavaScript code, you'll need a text editor, and to view your web page, you'll need a browser.

Chapter No 2: Working of JavaScript

2.1 Engine, the runtime, and the call stack

Teams utilize JavaScript's support on several levels in their stack, including front-end, backend, hybrid applications, embedded devices, and much more, as it becomes more mainstream.

It is the first in a series to delve deeper into JavaScript and how it works: we believe that understanding the building blocks of JavaScript and how they connect can help you write better code and applications. Some of the best practices used when developing SessionStack are a lightweight JavaScript framework that must be stable and quick to remain competitive.

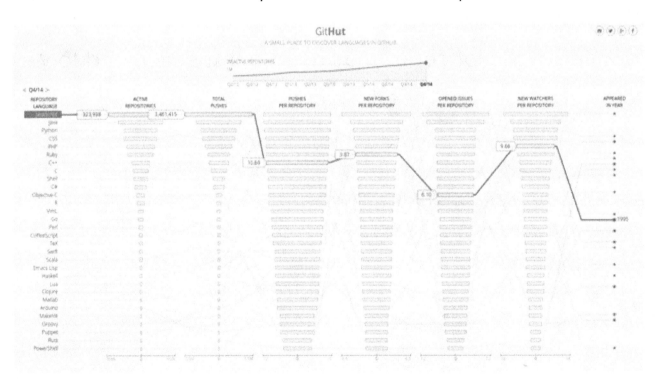

According to GitHub statistics, JavaScript has the most active repositories and total pushes on the platform. It also doesn't fall much away in the other groups.

Suppose projects are being increasingly dependent on JavaScript. In that case, developers must take advantage of all the language and ecosystem and better understand the internals to create fantastic software.

As it turns out, many developers use JavaScript regularly but are unaware of what occurs behind the scenes.

The V8 Engine is a concept that almost everybody is familiar with, and many people are aware that JavaScript uses a callback queue or is single-threaded.

This book will go through all of these topics in-depth and demonstrate how JavaScript works. You'll be able to write easier, non-blocking apps that use the given APIs properly if you know this information.

If you're new to JavaScript, this book would explain why the language is so "weird" compared to other languages.

Even if you're a professional JavaScript developer, it can provide you with some new insights into how the JavaScript Runtime you use everyday functions.

The JavaScript Engine

Google's V8 Engine is a typical example of a JavaScript Engine. Chrome and Node.js, for example, all use V8 Engine. Here's a simplified image of what it feels like:

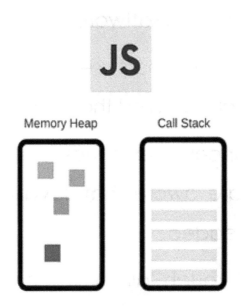

The Engine is made up of two major parts:

- Memory Heap — here is where memory is allocated

- Memory Heap — here is where memory is allocated

The Runtime

There are APIs in the browser that almost any JavaScript developer has used (for example, "setTimeout"). The Engine, on the other hand, does not have such APIs.

So, where do they originate?

The reality, it turns out, is a little more complex.

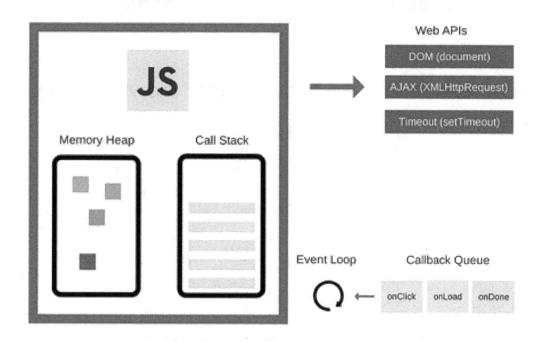

So, you've got the Engine, but there's a lot more. The DOM, AJAX, setTimeout, and other Web APIs are supported by browsers like the AJAX, DOM, and many more.

Then there's the event loop and the callback queue, which are all quite popular.

The Call Stack

Since JavaScript is a single-threaded programming language, it only has a single Call Stack. As a result, it can only do one task at a time.

The Call Stack is a data structure that keeps track of where you are in the application. You place a feature on top of the stack as it is talked through. You pop off the top of the stack when you return from a function. That's what the stack is capable of.

Let's see an example. Take a look at the following code:

```
function multiply(x, y)
{
    return x * y;
}
function printSquare(x)
{
    var s = multiply(x, x);
    console.log(s);
}
printSquare(5);
```

Call Stack becomes empty when the Engine begins running this code. The steps would be:

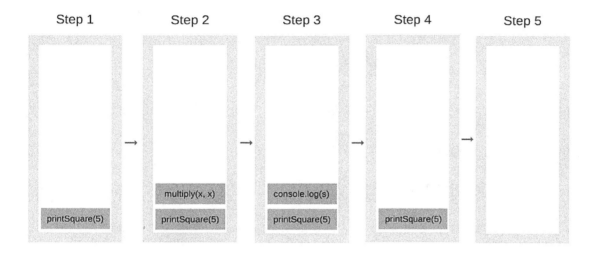

A Stack Frame is a term given to every entry in Call Stack.

And this is precisely how stack traces are built after an exception is thrown — it's essentially the condition of the Call Stack when the exception occurred. Have a look at the code below:

```
function foo()
{
    throw new Error('SessionStack will help you resolve crashes
:)');
}
function bar()
{
    foo();
}
function start()
{
    bar();
}
start();
```

If you run this code in Chrome (assuming it's in a file named foo.js), you'll get the following stack trace:

```
⊗ Uncaught Error: SessionStack will help you resolve crashes :) foo.js:2
    at foo (foo.js:2)
    at bar (foo.js:6)
    at start (foo.js:10)
    at foo.js:13
```

When you hit the full Call Stack size, this is known as "blowing the stack." And it could happen relatively quickly, mainly if you use recursion without thoroughly testing your code. Take a look at the following code:

```
function foo()
{
    foo();
}
foo();
```

The Engine begins by naming the function "foo" as it begins executing this code. On the other hand, this function is recursive and starts naming itself without any conditions for termination. As a result, the same feature is repeatedly applied to the Call Stack at each stage of the execution. It is what it seems to be like:

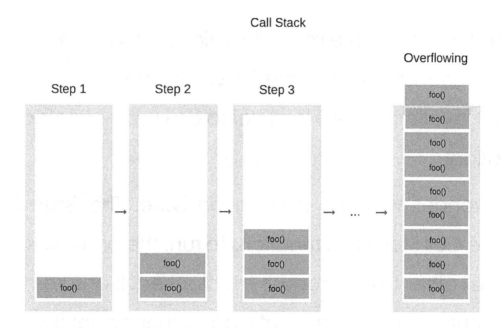

However, as the amount of function calls in the Call Stack reaches the Call Stack's actual size, the browser tries to intervene by throwing an error that looks something like this:

```
⊗ ▶ Uncaught RangeError: Maximum call stack size exceeded
```

Running code on a single thread is simple, so you don't have to deal with the complexities of multi-threaded systems, such as deadlocks.

However, operating on a single thread has its drawbacks. What occurs when things are slow in JavaScript because it only has a single Call Stack?

Concurrency & the Event Loop

What happens if you have many functions calls in the Call Stack that take a long time to process? Include the case where you want to use JavaScript in the browser to do a complicated image transformation.

You may wonder why this is even an issue. The issue is that, although the Call Stack has functions to run, the browser is unable to perform all other tasks because it is blocked. It ensures that the browser cannot render or execute any other code; it is stuck. It causes issues if you want the app to have excellent fluid UIs.

And it isn't the only problem. When your browser begins to process a large number of tasks in the Call Stack, it may become unresponsive for a long period. Most browsers respond by displaying an error message and asking you to choose whether to close the browser window.

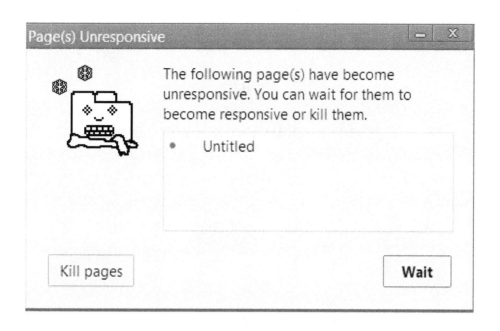

2.2 Working of JavaScript

It is a scripting language for interacting with the browser's GUI. Brendan Eich was the 1st to develop a JavaScript engine for Netspace's Navigator web browser. It was written in C and given the code name SpiderMonkey. The project was first known as Mocha, later renamed to LiveScript, and eventually renamed to JavaScript after Netspace and Sun reached a licensing agreement. You've probably heard of famous engines like Spider Monkey, V8, and plenty of others. For example, all engines have specific "codenames," such as:

- Opera and Chrome both use the V8 Engine.

- Firefox uses the SpiderMonkey engine.

- Engines used in IE and Nitro are the Trident and Chakra.

- Microsoft Edge uses the ChakraCore Engine.

- Safari uses the SquirrelFish Engine.

The JavaScript engine is made up of two key components:

- Heap Memory is the place where memory is allocated.

- The Call Stack is the location where the stacks are called, and the code is executed.

JavaScript is a single-threaded programming language, meaning it only has one Call Stack and can only do one thing simultaneously. The Call Stack is a data structure that keeps track of where the program is currently running. This call stack is comparable to other stacks in that it has simple features, such as putting a feature on top of the stack as you walk into it. If you want to return from a feature, you must pop off the top of the stack. Every stack's simple functionality is this. Although the engines that control JavaScript functions are extremely complex, the following are the simple tasks that each Engine executes in a broader sense:

- The Engine is embedded in the browser if the browser reads the document.

- It converts the script to machine language after reading it.

- Machine code then executes, and it does so quickly.

What will JavaScript do in the browser?

It modifies current content and styles by inserting new HTML into the pages.

Provides mouse click, mouse hover, and other functions that respond to the user's behavior.

Send and receive requests to remote servers over the network without loading the whole website as the user types. AJAX is a well-known example of such a technology.

It allows you to set and retrieve cookie values and send messages to users for information, alerts, and other purposes.

On the client-side, you can also store temporary data.

2.3 Restrictions in Browser

For the sake of the user's privacy, JavaScript's capabilities are restricted within the browser. The aim is to prohibit a third-party website from accessing personal information or causing damage to the user's data. The following are some examples of situations in which selective access is used:

JavaScript on a website is limited by design to reading/writing arbitrary files on the hard disc, copying them, and running programs. It doesn't even provide full access to the operating system's functions. Few modern browsers still allow it to work with files, but access is restricted and only granted if the user performs certain acts, such as "dropping" a file into a web browser. Some methods for interacting with the camera/microphone and other equipment are also possible, but they require the user's explicit permission. As a result, a JavaScript-enabled page cannot secretly activate a webcam or transfer data to a remote server or a third party.

In some instances, different tabs or windows are unaware of each other's existence. However, it is theoretically possible. The term for this is "Same Origin Policy." Both instances must have specific JavaScript code that can manage data sharing between them for the same to operate. However, the restriction is in place for the user's protection. For example, a web page from URL xyz.com that a user has opened must not be allowed to access information anonymously from another browser window with the URL abc.com.

It allows one to quickly connect over the Internet with every remote server or third party from which the current page originated. However, the ability to collect or transmit data from other pages or domains has been blocked for security purposes. However, some JavaScript works require tacit agreement from the remote side, which is still possible. If JavaScript is used outside of the window rather than within (from a server). Such a restriction would be impossible to implement. You will also note that specific modern browsers allow you to install plugins or extensions that give JavaScript within the browser more permissions.

2.4 Different from other scripting languages

- It's an object-based scripting language, as we all know.

- It is written in the C programming language. It's a language that's been interpreted.

- When it comes to DOM entry, pure JavaScript is faster.

- The user has greater power over the browser when JavaScript is used.

- It also works for dates and timestamps.

- It can also identify the user's browser and operating system.

- It is lightweight.

- It is, as previously mentioned, a scripting language.

- It is a scripting language that uses an interpreter.

- It is case sensitive in the sense that the grammar is case sensitive.

- It is an object-oriented language because it provides predefined objects, similar to Java, but not Java.

- A semicolon must be used to end each statement in JavaScript (;).

- The ability to generate new functions inside scripts is the most valuable feature provided by JavaScript. The function keyword in JavaScript can be used to declare a function.

- HTML and CSS are also fully supported.

- It is very simple to use.

- Both web browsers are supported.

2.5 Limitations

Among its many benefits, JavaScript has a few drawbacks, which are mentioned below:

- JavaScript is a client-side script that does not support reading or writing files to disc.

- Since it lacks networking support, JavaScript cannot be used in networking applications.

- It does not support multithreading or multiprocessing.

Note

As a result, we all learned about some fundamental facts about JavaScript's development, some of the well-known engines that run JavaScript on web browsers, the benefits of having JavaScript within browsers. You've also discovered some of the features of JavaScript's work that make it valuable and unique. There are some of its limitations and drawbacks.

Chapter No 3: Basic Rules and Practical Application

3.1 Basic rules of JavaScript

The following rules apply to the basic syntax of JavaScript:

1. Variable, Object, and Function Names

Before being used, it must be defined. The variable name may begin with a letter or an underscore ("_") and may include A–Z, a–z, underscore, or digits.

Assume the data form that will be entered into the variable. The data form does not need to be specified explicitly.

When specified outside of a function, global variables are accessible anywhere in the current script context. Local variables are variables created within a function that can only be used within the function.

Quotation marks, either single or double, must be used to enclose strings. For instance, print(" Hello" + 'world '+ Country.name) results in 'Hello world America'.

A backslash character must come before any special characters that are shown literally (\). A backslash may also be used to precede quotes within a series.

You will use a++ to increment a variable, such as a = a + 1. In the same way as a—, you can decrement a variable.

Using "//" to begin a single-line comment or a mixture of "/*" and "*/" to enclose a multi-line comment in the script.

Date, Array, Boolean, String, and Number are examples of objects that aren't specified as data types (string, number, and Boolean). For instance, you might write: var ArrayList=new Array("test", "this", "list");

In JavaScript, dots in Service Manager field names must be substituted by an underscore (_). For instance, contact.name is changed to contact_name.

Reserved terms in JavaScript, such as "_class" for the "class" sector, must be followed by an underscore in Service Manager field names.

You get to name your variables, objects, and functions when you create them. Uppercase characters, lowercase letters, numbers, and the underscore (_) character will all be used in names. The first character in a name must be a letter or an underscore.

You can use caps or lowercase in the variable names, but keep in mind that JavaScript is case sensitive, so score, Score, and

SCORE are all three separate variables. Make sure you always refer to a variable with the same name every time.

2. Syntax Rules for JavaScript

While JavaScript is a simple language, you must be careful to follow its syntax (the rules that govern how you use it). Numerous aspects of JavaScript syntax are discussed in the rest of this book, but you should know a few simple rules to prevent errors.

3. Case Sensitivity

Almost everything in JavaScript is case-sensitive, which means you can't mix lowercase and capital letters. Here are few general guidelines:

- Lowercase keywords in JavaScript, like for and if, are often used.

- Math and Date are built-in objects that are capitalized.

- The names of DOM objects are usually lowercase, but their methods are often a mix of capitals and lowercase. All except the first word is usually capitalized, as in toLowerCase & getElementById.

The browser will normally show an error message if you choose the incorrect example.

4. Reserved Words

Another requirement for variable names is that they do not contain reserved words. These include JavaScript language terms like if and for, DOM object names like window and document, and built-in object names like Math and Date and DOM object names like window and document. Appendix D, "JavaScript Quick Reference," contains a comprehensive list of reserved terms.

5. Spacing

JavaScript disregards whitespace (also known as blank space in programming). Without creating an error, you can include spaces, tabs, and blank lines within a line. The use of white space improves the readability of a script.

3.2 JavaScript Applications – JavaScript Uses in Web Designing

All over the world, JavaScript is the most commonly used programming language. It has the world's most extensive open-source package repository (npm). JavaScript is used for any program, including server code (Node.js), productivity applications, 3D games, robots, and IoT devices. JavaScript accomplished Java's aim several years ago: write once, run anywhere. Let's take a look at how JavaScript is used in different segments one by one.

JavaScript Applications

According to a new Stack Overflow survey, JavaScript is the most common programming language on the planet. What's interesting about these survey findings is that even developers whose main responsibility is the backend (server-side code) are more inclined than any other language to study questions about JavaScript. It is because JavaScript is unavoidable. All of our Java or.NET Bootcamp students will inform you that one of their final projects required them to learn JavaScript at a simple level. It is true in the workplace as well. Any teams without dedicated front-end developers would have to do so on their own. Any program that can be written in JavaScript can also be written in JavaScript.

Jeff Atwood was joking about JavaScript, but it turned out to be more accurate than not. With advancements in browser technologies and JavaScript's transition to the server with NodeJS, JavaScript can now do a lot more than it could a few years earlier. Here's a fast rundown on what JavaScript can do for you. Some of it is self-evident, although others are not so.

JavaScript is mainly used in the following:

1. Websites

JavaScript allows you to add behavior to a web page to respond to user behaviors without requiring the user to load a new page to process the request. It helps the website to communicate with users and carry out complex tasks.

So, this one falls under the category of "pretty obvious." Brendan Eich developed JavaScript in 1995, created it to add interactivity and actions to otherwise static websites. That's what it's still used for. It is a simple one. On some level, any modern website runs JavaScript. It is a gimme.

2. Web Applications

JavaScript has developed the ability to build robust web applications as browsers and computers have improved. Take a look at Google Maps, for instance. Click and drag with your mouse to discover a map in Google Maps. You'll see the less accurate part of the map until it fills up on its own. JavaScript is responsible for all of this.

3. Presentations

The creation of presentations as websites is a popular JavaScript application. If you're familiar with HTML and CSS, you can do this quickly using the Reveal.js framework. The development of presentations as websites is a common use of JavaScript. Who wants Keynote or PowerPoint? If you're already familiar with HTML and CSS, using the RevealJS library makes this easy. If you're not familiar with these methods, you can also use slides.com to create a web-based slide deck for you, which uses RevealJS.

4. Web Servers

Node or Express.js (the server application framework) will help you build even more reliable servers. The Mongo Express Angular Node stack (MEAN), of which Express is a key component, constructs most of the previously described Nodes.

5. Server Applications

JavaScript was moved from the desktop to the server with the introduction of Node.js a few years back. Since then, large corporations like Wal-Mart have implemented Node as a critical component of their backend infrastructure.

6. Art

The canvas module, which enables the browser to make three-dimensional spaces, is one of the latest features of the HTML5 specification. It makes the browser-accessible as a new source of digital art projects.

7. Games

The browser hasn't always been the traditional platform for games. It has recently proven to be very capable. Furthermore, the level of complexity that can be achieved in browser-based gaming has increased exponentially with the inclusion of HTML5 canvas. Even browser games that teach us how to code are available.

8. Smart watch Apps

Pebble.js is a small and simple JavaScript framework that allows developers to write Pebble watch applications in JavaScript.

9. Mobile Apps

Creating an app for non-web contexts is one of the most powerful things one can do with JavaScript. You can build applications for items that aren't available on the Internet. Building applications for non-web contexts is one of the most powerful things anyone can do with JavaScript. That's a fancy way of suggesting you should create applications that aren't related to the Internet. Mobile devices, for example, are now the most common means of accessing the Internet. It means that all of the websites should be mobile-friendly. Furthermore, it implies that smartphone apps are just as important as web properties for digital goods. The catch is that there are two types of mobile apps: Apple and Android.

Moreover, the apps are written in 2 different languages. To create and maintain an app for mobile devices and the Internet, you'll need 3 times as many developers. The positive news is that a "write it once" approach for all 3 platforms is feasible. Phonegap is one of the most well-established and well-known frameworks in this field. React Native has recently emerged on the scene and appears to have many potentials to become a significant player in the cross-platform market. To cut a long story short, you can use JavaScript to create smartphone applications that you can deploy and import from the respective app stores.

10. Flying Robots

That's right. You read that correctly. Node.js can be installed on many commercially available quadcopters, some of which come with a basic operating system. It means you can use JavaScript to program a flying robot. JavaScript is the most user-friendly programming language on the planet, with a wide range of capabilities. It's encouraging to see that it's generating such a diverse set of applications.

3.3 Importance of JavaScript in Web Designing

Explore the various features of JavaScript. Importance of JavaScript in Web Designing. There are different web designing and practical uses of JavaScript:

1. Improvement of the Web Interface

You use JavaScript these days to make the old, tired, and real web interface – clicking links, entering content, and sending it off, for example – more accessible to the end-user. For instance, a sign-up form will check if your name is available before you enter it, saving you the trouble of having to reload the page.

2. Recommended Words in the Search Box

It will suggest results based on what you've already typed when you type in a search box.

For example, the string "bi" might generate a list of suggestions that include words like "bird," "big," and "bicycle." Autocomplete is the name of this usage pattern. Information that varies often can be loaded regularly without requiring user intervention.

For instance, stock market tickers or sports match scores.

3. Loading Information Only When User Choose

Information that is useful but could be unnecessary for other users can be loaded when and where they request it. E.g., a site's navigation menu can contain six links, but links to deeper pages are shown on demand when a menu item is enabled. Don't forget to look over JavaScript Syntax 5 as well.

4. Fixing Layout Issues

It will determine the element's location and area on a specific page, as well as the browser window's dimensions. You can avoid overlapping elements as well as other problems by using this material.

5. Enhancing HTML Interface

The HTML interfaces can be enhanced with JavaScript. Although a text input box is useful, you might choose a combo box that allows you to choose from a list of preset values or add your own. You can enhance the normal input box to do so using JavaScript.

6. Animation of Page Elements

JavaScript allows you to animate objects on a website to show and hide data and highlight specific parts of a page, making it more accessible and providing a richer user experience.

In this chapter, you looked at how JavaScript can be used in various fields, like web design. There are several other uses for JavaScript that help in enhancing the functionality of web pages and the user interface.

3.4 JavaScript Projects for Beginners

These JavaScript project ideas for beginners are samples of things you can code with basic JavaScript skills (with some CSS and HTML). Through studying the source code for both of these basic JavaScript projects, you'll be able to see how you might create your variant of the same concept or improve on the initial open-source code and add your specific twists & tweaks.

1. Build a JavaScript clock

There's a decent possibility that if you're on a website or using a web application that has a self-updating time function (like a clock), it's driven by JavaScript code. It means that JavaScript clocks aren't just helpful in creating JavaScript projects; they also allow you to practice the type of work you'll be doing as a JavaScript developer.

2. Build a JavaScript tip calculator

You fumble for the phone and look for a "tip calculator" on Google if you go out to eat and have trouble measuring the correct tip. The one you usually use doesn't have a name or a URL, but it's a basic JavaScript program. So go ahead and build your tip calculator.

3. Build a JavaScript animated navigation toggle

When using HTML and CSS to create website menus, you're restricted to making links that transfer the user from 1 static page to another—JavaScript is what makes for drop-down, collapsible, and other animated navigation features in web creation. Animated navigation toggles are yet another popular feature of the Internet that you'll be able to create for clients and future employers once you've mastered the JavaScript programming language.

4. Build a JavaScript map

If you've used Google Maps to zoom in on the spot or change your view mode, you've used JavaScript-based features. Because of JavaScript's ability to generate complex objects, it's a perfect match for creating innovative interactive maps for websites or mobile apps.

5. Build a JavaScript game

While HTML and CSS are essential building blocks in web creation, JavaScript is the programming language that transforms websites from functionality to entertainment. It's no wonder. Then, those games are among the entertaining JavaScript projects that allow you to refine your skills without taking a nap at the keyboard.

6. Build a mouseover element

When hovering a mouse over a specific icon or region on a page creates an event or outcome from the location where you're hovering—it is another piece of JavaScript goodness you've grown to rely on online. Since mouseovers are a basic feature of JavaScript development, spending an afternoon working on a simple mouseover JavaScript task is a good way to pass the time.

7. Build a JavaScript login authentication

Another part of JavaScript's domain is a website's sign-in authentication bar (a place where you type your email & password to sign in to the site). Since almost every site has a login authentication feature, this JavaScript project for newcomers is a good idea to master.

8. Build a JavaScript drawing

JavaScript could be used as a drawing medium to put HTML & CSS elements to life on a web browser screen. Adding graphical elements to static websites is an essential aspect of web creation, so understanding how to use JavaScript's drawing capability is vital.

9. Build a JavaScript to-do list

JavaScript is beneficial for creating dynamic lists that allow users to add, delete, and group items—something that CSS and HTML alone cannot do. If you mean to make a to-do list but never get around to it, now's your opportunity. Make a to-do list for your JavaScript skills.

10. Build a JavaScript quiz

Who doesn't like a good quiz? Quizzes could be both fun and useful, whether they're determining which career direction you're better suited for, where the political views align or checking your knowledge of 1980's WWF wrestlers. If you've ever taken an online quiz, there's a fair chance any JavaScript source code was used, and now's your opportunity to create your quiz.

11. Create some sliding JavaScript drawers

Pushbar.js is a JavaScript module that helps developers add "sliding drawer" menus to their website or app (menus that can be dragged onscreen from the bottom, top, or left and right of an app).

3.5 Advanced JavaScript Projects

You may be wondering what more JavaScript advanced projects look like after you've become comfortable with the basic JavaScript projects mentioned above. Here are some advanced JavaScript projects that go beyond the basics but are also open source, so you can learn the code and see how it all works and then try your hand at something similar.

1. Prettier

Prettier is an "opinionated JavaScript formatter," which means it's a JavaScript program that removes all of the JavaScript code's original styling and replaces it with a single, prettier standard style.

2. Terminalizer

Terminalizer is a fast, open-source project of JavaScript that records the terminal screen and converts it into an animated gif—ideal for terminal tutorials and demos.

3. Nano id

Need a random Identification number for something important, like your bank account information (or don't want your roommate watching Netflix)? Nano ID is a JavaScript program that generates IDs at random. It will take 149 billion years for a 1% chance of at least one collision to occur. In other words, your roommate would have a hard time guessing.

4. Reaction

The reaction is a brilliant example of how far JavaScript will take you. It raises the bar from a JavaScript project that assists with a single type of transaction to a JavaScript project that enables users to manage an entire business. The reaction is a commerce network for real-time handling business and providing direct shopping experiences to consumers. It's all open-source, so you can look at how it all functions!

5. Webpack monitor

Webpack Monitor is a high-level, open-source JavaScript framework that aims to enhance the overall user interface of applications. This JavaScript program monitors the size and consistency of an application's "bundle" to ensure that it runs smoothly.

6. Maptalks

Maptalks is a much more advanced JavaScript project example that builds on the previous basic JavaScript map project. Maptalks combines 2D and 3D maps to create shifting, animated landscapes with the ability to extrude and flatten buildings and terrain at will.

7. Ar.js

AR.js is a JavaScript project that attempts to introduce the virtual reality experience to smartphones using JavaScript.

8. Parcel

The parcel is a JavaScript application bundler that can quickly assemble all of an application's files and assets. What gives that this is possible? Investigate the code for yourself to see what you can do!

9. Workbox

Workbox is a series of JavaScript libraries that enable web apps to provide offline capabilities. If any app uses Workbox, you won't be as disappointed the next time the Wi-Fi goes out.

10. Tone.js

Tone.js is a JavaScript framework that allows you to make immersive music in your web browser. Advanced scheduling, effects and synths, and intuitive musical abstractions developed on top of the Web Audio API are included.

Chapter 4. Writing Your First JavaScript Program

HTML doesn't have any intelligence of its own: it can't do the math, can't tell whether anyone has filled out a form right, and can't make choices depending on how a page user interacts with it. HTML allows users to read text, look at images, watch videos, and navigate to other web pages containing more pictures, text, and videos by clicking links. JavaScript is used to add intelligence to the web pages to react to the site's visitors.

JavaScript allows a website to react intelligently. You may use it to build smart web forms that warn users when they've forgotten to fill in required details. A web page's elements may be made to appear, disappear, or move about. You may also use information obtained from a web server to refresh the parts of a web page without reloading it. In a nutshell, JavaScript allows you to improve your website's engagement, effectiveness, and usefulness.

Note

HTML5 does, in reality, apply some intelligence to HTML, including simple type validation. However, since not all browsers accept these handy additions (and because forms and JavaScript can do so many more), JavaScript is still required to create the safest, most user-friendly, and interactive types.

4.1 Programming Introduction

For certain people, the phrase "computer programming" conjures up images of intelligent programmers hunched over the keyboards for hours on end, typing almost unintelligible gibberish. And, to tell you the truth, some programming is like that. Programming may seem to be a sophisticated form of magic outside the grasp of the ordinary mortal. However, many programming principles are simple to understand, and JavaScript is a decent first programming language for anyone new to programming.

Even JavaScript is more complicated than HTML or CSS, and scripting is always a foreign environment to web designers; hence, this book aims to teach you how to think like a programmer. You'll discover basic programming principles in this book that matter when you're writing JavaScript. You'll also learn how to handle a programming challenge to know what you want to do when applying JavaScript to a new website.

The strange symbols and vocabulary used in JavaScript strike many web designers as strange. A typical JavaScript program is littered with symbols ({}, [ ], ; , ()!=), as well as a slew of unfamiliar terms (null, var, else if). Learning a programming language is similar to learning another language in several respects. It would help if you learned new words, punctuation, and how to bring them together to communicate effectively.

Every programming language has its collection of characters and keywords and its syntax (the rules for bringing certain words and characters together). You'll need to memorize the JavaScript language's terms and regulations. When learning a foreign language, it's easy to forget that emphasizing the wrong syllable will make a word unintelligible. A fundamental mistake or even a missed punctuation mark may prevent a JavaScript program from running or triggering a web browser crash. You'll make lots of errors when you learn to program—it's the essence of programming to make mistakes.

You'll find JavaScript programming boring at first since you'll waste a lot of time looking for mistakes you made when writing the script. You might also find some of the programming terms challenging to follow at first. But don't worry: if you've tried to learn JavaScript before and given up because you felt it was too complicated, this book will guide you through the standard stumbling blocks that new programmers face. (Even though you have prior programming knowledge, this book will show you JavaScript's characteristics and the particular principles involved with web browser programming.)

4.2 Computer Program

You're writing a computer program when you apply JavaScript to a web page. Most JavaScript applications are far easier to use than the programs you use to read email, retouch photos, or create web pages. Although JavaScript programs (also known as scripts) are more straightforward and shorter than more complex programs, they have much of the same properties.

A computer program is a collection of instructions followed in a specific sequence in a nutshell. Let's say you want to show a greeting note that includes the visitor's name: "Welcome, Bob!" To complete this mission, you would need to do the following:

- Ask the visitor's name.

- Get the visitor's response.

- Print (that is, display) the message on the web page.

Although you would never choose to print a welcome message on a web page, this illustration shows the basic programming process: Determine what you intend to do, and break it down into small steps. Whenever you try to make a JavaScript application, you must first figure out what measures you need to accomplish your task. If you've mastered the steps, you'll be able to convert your thoughts into computer code—the terms and characters that tell the web browser how to behave.

4.3 Adding JavaScript to a Page

Web browsers are designed to interpret HTML and CSS and translate them into visual representations on the page. The layout or rendering engine is the component of the internet browser that understands HTML and CSS. However, most browsers still have a JavaScript interpreter. It is the portion of the browser that knows JavaScript and can run a JavaScript application. Since most web browsers anticipate HTML, you must use the <script> tag to explicitly inform the browser that JavaScript is arriving.

The <script> tag is a standard HTML tag. It functions like a switch that says, "Hey, web browser, here's some JavaScript code; you have no idea what to do about it, so pass it over to the JavaScript interpreter." As the web browser sees the closing </script> tag, it realizes it's finished with the JavaScript program and can return to its regular tasks.

In most cases, you'll include the <script> tag in the <head> section of the web page, as seen here:

```
<!DOCTYPE HTML PUBLIC "-//W3C//DTD HTML 4.01//EN" "http://www.w3.org/TR/
html4/strict.dtd">
<html>
<head>
<title>My Web Page</title>
<script type="text/javascript">
</script>
</head>
```

The style attribute of the <script> tag specifies the structure and type of script that follows. For this case, type= "text/JavaScript" denotes that the script is plain text (as opposed to HTML) and written in JavaScript.

It's much easier if you're using HTML5. You should entirely exclude the class attribute:

```
<!doctype html>
<html>
<head>
<meta charset="UTF-8">
<title>My Web Page</title>
<script>
</script>
</head>
```

In reality, web browsers allow you to remove the form attribute from HTML 4.01 & XHTML 1.0 files—the script will still run; but, your website will not validate properly without it. The doctype in this book is HTML5, but the JavaScript version is the same and works with HTML 4.01 and XHTML 1.

Then, between the opening & closing <script> tags, add the JavaScript code:

```html
<!doctype html>
<html>
<head>
<meta charset="UTF-8">
<title>My Web Page</title>
<script>
  alert('hello world!');
</script>
</head>
```

In a moment, you'll see what this JavaScript does. For the time being, concentrate on the opening & closing <script> tags. Start by adding these tags to add the script to the website. In certain instances, you'll include the <script> tags in the page's <head> to hold your JavaScript code nicely arranged in one area.

<script> tags, on the other hand, maybe placed anywhere in the HTML of a website. In reality, as you'll see later in the chapter, JavaScript has a command that allows you to write data directly into a web page. The <script> tags are placed in the spot on the page (somewhere within the body) where you want the script to create its message using that command. In reality, it's normal to place <script> tags just below the closing </body> tag, as this ensures that the page is loaded and visible to the visitor before running any JavaScript.

External JavaScript Files

You may apply JavaScript to a single website using the <script> tag, as mentioned in the previous section. However, you'll often build scripts that you'd like to post through all of your site's pages. You may, for example, add a panel of extra navigation choices that slides into the page in reaction to a visitor's mouse movements. While you'll like the similar fancy slide-in panel on each page of the site, copying & pasting the similar JavaScript code into every page is a terrible idea for many purposes.

First, copying & pasting the same code over & over takes a lot of time, particularly if you have a large site with 100s of pages. Second, if you wish to modify or improve the JavaScript version, you'll need to find and upgrade the code for any website that uses it. Finally, since a web page would include all of the JavaScript program's code, each page would be significantly larger and longer to download.

Using an external JavaScript file is a better option. If you've ever used external CSS files for the websites, you'll be familiar with this process. An external JavaScript file is a text file that contains JavaScript code and ends in.js (for example, navigation.js). The <script> tag is used to connect the file to a web page. You might, for example, write the following to link this JavaScript file to the home page:

```
<!doctype html>
<html>
<head>
<meta charset="UTF-8">
<title>My Web Page</title>
<script src="navigation.js"></script>
</head>
```

The src attribute of the <script> tag functions similarly to the src attribute of an <img> tag or the href attribute of an <a> tag. In other terms, it directs visitors to a file on your or another website.

4.4 Hello World JavaScript Program

In computer technology, the "Hello, World!" program is a popular and time-honored practice. It's a simple and comprehensive first program for newcomers, and it's a fantastic way to ensure the environment is set up correctly.

This book will help you how to write a JavaScript program. Make the program more interesting; a question is added to the standard "Hello, World!" application that asks for the user's name. The name would then be included as a greeting. You'll have an immersive "Hello, World!" program when you finish this.

Prerequisites

Using the JavaScript Developer Console in the web browser, you will finish this tutorial. It would help if you got some experience working with this method before starting this tutorial.

Creating the "Hello, World!" Program

To write the "Hello, World!" program, open the JavaScript Console in your preferred web browser.

The alert() method and the console.log() method are the two primary ways in which we can build the "Hello, World!" program in JavaScript.

Using alert()

The alert() method can be used to show an alert box over the current window with a given message (in this case, "Hello, World!") and an OK button that allows the user to close the notification.

It'll transfer the string data form as a parameter to the function. The value of the string will be Hello, World!, and it will be printed in the alert box.

We'll encase the string inside the parentheses of the alert() method to compose this first type of "Hello, World!" program. A semicolon would be used to finish our JavaScript statement.

```
alert("Hello, World!");
```

You will see the following alert show up in your window after pressing the ENTER key after your line of JavaScript:

JavaScript Console Alert Example

Testing an expression will also be printed in the Console. It will read as ambiguous if the expression doesn't return anything.

It can be frustrating to keep clicking out of popup alerts, but let's look at making the same program via logging it to Dashboard with console.log ().

Using console.log()

You may use the console.log() method to print a similar string, but this time to the JavaScript console. Using this option is identical to using a programming language in a terminal environment on your computer.

You'll send the "Hello, World!" string to a console.log() method between parentheses, much as we did with alert(). As is standard in JavaScript syntax, you'll finish the sentence with a semicolon.

```
console.log("Hello, World!");
```

'Hello, World!' text will be displayed to the Console when you click ENTER:

```
Output
Hello, World!
```

Prompting for Input

The quality of the current "Hello, World!" program is the same every time you run it. Let's get the name of the guy who's operating the program. The output can then be customized with that name.

You may start with a single line prompting for input for each of the JavaScript techniques used above. To ask the user for their name, you'll use JavaScript's prompt() method and pass it the string as shown below "What is your name?" The user's input would then be saved in the variable term. You'll put a semicolon at the end of the expression.

```
let name = prompt("What is your name?");
```

You'll get a popup prompt when you click ENTER to execute this line of code:

What is your name?

| |

Cancel   OK

JavaScript Prompt Example

A text field appears in the dialogue box that appears over the web browser window, allowing the user to enter information. Once the user has entered a value in the text field, they must press OK to save the value. By pressing the Cancel icon, the user may also prevent the value from being recorded.

It's necessary to use the JavaScript prompt() method when it makes sense in the program's background; otherwise, the user may get tired of it.

Enter the name you want the program to greet you with at this stage. Let's use Sammy in this case.

Now that you've gathered the meaning of the user's name, you can use the value to welcome the user.

Greeting the user with an alert()

The alert() method, as previously mentioned, produces a popup screen over the browser window. Using the variable name, you will use the technique to welcome the recipient.

You'll use string concatenation to write a greeting that says "Hello!" to the user directly. So, let's concatenate the Hello string with the name variable:

```
"Hello, " + name + "!"
```

With the name variable in between, combine two strings, "Hello" and "!" This expression can now be passed to the alert() method.

```
alert("Hello, " + name + "!");
```

When you click ENTER here, the following dialogue box will appear on the screen:

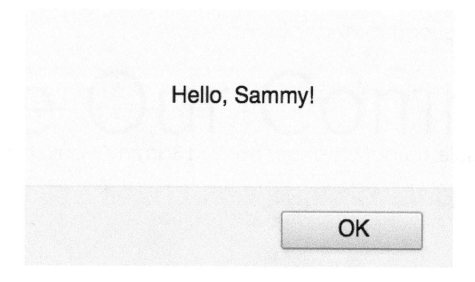

Since the user's name is Sammy in this situation, the output has mentioned him.

Let's rewrite this such that the output is instead printed to the Console.

Greeting the user with console.log()

The console.log() method, as you saw in the previous section, prints output to a Console, similar to how the print() function in Python will print output to the terminal.

You'll use the exact concatenated string you used for the alert() method, which includes the strings "Hello," & "!" as well as the name variable:

```
"Hello, " + name + "!"
```

The Console's parentheses would be used to contain the whole expression. So that we get a greeting as output, you'll use the console.log() method.

```
console.log("Hello, " + name + "!");
```

The Console output for a user named Sammy would be as follows:

```
Output

Hello, Sammy!
```

You have a JavaScript program that accepts user input and prints it to the screen.

You will now focus on expanding the program to understand how to write the famous "Hello, World!" program and alert the user for input and show it as output. For example, if you ask the user for their favorite color, the program would respond that their favorite color is red. You might also try your hand at making a Mad Lib program using this method.

Chapter No 5: JavaScript Mistakes to Avoid

Designers want to eliminate a few typical programming errors to keep the code safe and readable. You'll look into each one in this chapter and how to stop them.

1. Too Many Things in One Function

One function can do one thing: whatever is defined on its own, if something else can be moved to a separate function. It isn't easy to read & follow a function with so many things in it. If a function returns both the subtotal & the taxes, they can be split into two separate functions because they are different.

2. Commented-Out Code

Code that is commented out will not run. As a result, after you've finished working on that section of the code, they shouldn't be there. You can delete or uncomment the commented-out lines until you're done.

In any case, commented-out code should not exist in the final product.

3. Variable Names That Aren't Descriptive

When you forget about the code you wrote and come back to it, you get frustrated because you named variables in ways that don't express their meaning.

As a result, you can give variables names that define what they contain.

Rather than writing 'let x;', you can write let numApples; to ensure that the variable holds the number of apples.

4. Magic Numbers and String

There should be no magic numbers or strings. Some values occur in different places and say the same thing, but the code doesn't explain it explicitly.

For example, consider the following code:

```
for (let i = 0; i < 10; i++) {
  ///...
}
```

Then you have no idea what the 10 means. Instead, you can make it a named constant so you can understand what it is.

For example, you can write:

```
const numApples = 10;
for (let i = 0; i < numApples; i++) {
  ///...
}
```

Now you know that 10 means the no. of apples.

5. Messy Code Formatting

Since messy code formatting makes it difficult to read, you can use a code formatter or linter to clean it up. There are several options available, so you can use something like ESLint or Prettier to do the tidying for you.

6. Hard Coding Values

You should never hard code values, particularly if they are secrets, into the code. Instead, you can save those as environment variables from which you can read all the values. There are several ways to do so. For example, Vue, React, and Angular all have places to store variables for various environments in different files for the front end.

You will use the dotenv package to interpret environment variables from a .env file instead of hard coding them in the back end. It would help if you didn't look in the .env file because you don't want secrets in the code repositories.

7. Repetitive Code

It's a terrible idea to use the programming that repeats itself. If you adjust everything that repeats, you must change it everywhere. Rather, you can separate the common sections into their file so that they can be reused.

The theory of DRY (do not repeat yourself) applies to all situations. You can move them to a shared place if you are copying and pasting them & using them exactly as is.

8. Not Backing Up Code

You should use Git to manage the code because it allows you to have both a local & remote repo for the code.

It allows you to automatically store one copy in a remote location. You can also quickly remove bad code and restore code from earlier commits. Without version control, you won't be able to accomplish this. You could lose everything if anything goes wrong if you don't have the code backed up.

9. Complicated Code

Complex code must be simplified to make it easier to understand.

We can also split them down into smaller components to reuse stuff and provide individual sections that are simple to read & test.

These popular blunders can be easily avoided if you pay attention to what you're doing.

It's always a good idea to break things down into small bits and keep it clear and avoid repetition.

Variables & values that aren't descriptive should be replaced with something more meaningful, and variables & values that aren't commented out should be removed.

10. The "+" Symbol Is for Addition and Concatenation

In most programming languages, the "+" symbol is different for both addition & concatenation; however, this is not the case in JavaScript. When writing sentences with the "+" symbol, extra caution is needed.

Because of user feedback, you mix strings and numbers while using JavaScript. Since 7 is a string, and the + sign converts to a concatenation symbol if you're dealing with strings in JavaScript, the code var x = 20 + "7" gives "207." Once submission values are imputed, it's easy to forget that now the user input could be evaluated as a string, which leads to this mistake.

To avoid making this common mistake, convert the string number to an integer. For example, var x = 20 + parseInt("7", 20); in this case, the string number is parsed to an integer value of 7, and addition is used instead of concatenation.

11. Incorrect Use Of "If" Statement Comparison Operator

Professional JavaScript programmers often make the mistake of using the "if" statement comparison operator incorrectly. Even if it appears in your code as a minor typographical mistake, it may result in a significant logic bug after you've finished coding. As a result, you must be extremely careful to avoid making this error.

The operators "==" and "=" are used in Java Scripting. The "=" is used to assign a variable value, while the "==" operator is used to make a comparison. Using such operators in other programming languages can result in an error, but in JavaScript, it is evaluated, and you get a statement result that reads true or false.

If you write the statement: var x = 0; if (x == 4) to JavaScript, it will be read as valid, and it will correctly evaluate if x equals 4.

However, in the case of an incorrect imputation, such as var x = 0; if (x = 5), the 'if' statement contains a typographical error. The assigned operator is used instead of the comparison operator. In the other programming languages, this will be interpreted as a mistake, but not in JavaScript. Though such errors can be identified by testing, it's best to use a comparison operator for your 'if' statements all of the time.

12. No Block-Level Scope on JavaScript

You can describe a variable for the loop structure in many languages. If you use JavaScript to loop around a variable, the loop would be broken.

Consider the following scenario:

Where (var k = 0; k < 11; k++) { k = k + 1; } console.log (k); even the most advanced developers will presume that "k" is null when faced with code like this. The k variable is frequently used in the "for" loop in other programming languages, but it is destroyed when the loop is completed.

When JavaScript displays the product of the above code, it displays the value of the k variable as 10. As a new JavaScript developer, it's easy to ignore this language quirk that isn't seen in other programming languages, which could result in serious bugs in your code.

13. Using Named Object Indexes as Arrays Isn't a Good Idea

Numeric integers are used in JavaScript arrays. Similarly, objects can be used in the same way that arrays are, though the indexes would have to be named. However, if a named index is being used in an array, the output of the code will be incorrect.

For example:

var color = [];

color[0] = "black";

color[1] = "grey";

color[2] = "yellow";

var a = color.length;

var b = color [0];

The array is in "color" in the code above. Colors have been allocated to the first three variables; the length has been measured. The first color has now been assigned to variable b. The variable a would then be set to 3, and the value "black" is assigned to the variable b. It is a typical array pattern.

For the second example, we have created an object using a mobile

var mobile = [];

```
mobile ["color"] = "black";

mobile ["make"] = "samsung";

mobile ["model"] = "note";

var a = mobile.length;

var b = mobile [0];
```

The second code defines the object. You can tell it's an entity rather than an array because of the labeled indexes. Three named indexes describe the mobile. Variables a and b are the cause of the error. The values in the 2nd code, unlike the code with the array, are undefined and generate invalid results. The length property is set to 0, and the value of b is set to "undefined."

When working with these 2 data forms, it's essential to understand which one you're dealing with so you can use the correct calculations and properties.

14. Reference To "This" Correctly

The use of self-referencing scopes in callbacks and closures has become more popular. Along with the power of meaning, they are a frequent source of "this/that" confusion. You'll get the error message if you make this mistake.

The typical approach to this error is to save the reference "this" in a variable that the closure will quickly inherit; this solution works well in older browsers. In newer browsers, the "bind()" method is used to provide a proper reference.

15. Don't Mix-up Undefined and Null

Variables can be set to null in some programming languages; on the other hand, JavaScript uses undefined & null. Objects and variables in JavaScript are often set to null by default. Once these values are assigned, there are two scenarios:

- A mistake was found in the calculation.

- An object was assigned a null reference.

When comparing objects, be careful for an object must be defined for it to be null.

For example:

```
if (object !== null && type of object !== "undefined")
```

You'll get an error if the object can't be identified. To determine whether an object is null, you must first determine if it is undefined or not:

```
if (type of object !== "undefined" && object!== null)
```

Being careful is important to get the correct results.

16. DOM-related

The Document Object Model (DOM) is a crucial component of website interactivity. The DOM GUI allows you to control the text, design, and layout of a web page. The JavaScript scripting language was created for the sole purpose of making simple Html websites interactive (or controlling the DOM).

Working with the DOM is already a huge part of what JavaScript does, particularly with the advent of backend JavaScript technology like Node.js. As a result, the DOM may be a major source of bugs & errors in JavaScript apps.

It's no wonder that the JavaScript error report analysis discovered that DOM-related problems account for 68 percent of the flaws.

Some JavaScript programmers, for example, often make the error of referencing a DOM feature before it has been loaded, resulting in code errors.

```
<!DOCTYPE html>
<html>
<body>
<script>
document.getElementById("container").innerHTML = "Common JS
Bugs and Errors";
</script>
<div id="container"></div>
</body>
</html>
Copy
```

If you run the code above in Chrome, you'll get the following error message in the developer console:

Since JavaScript code is typically executed to occur on a document, the error is thrown. As a result, the browser is ignorant of referenced <div> element when the code runs.

You may use a variety of methods to solve such an issue. The most straightforward approach is to put the <div id="container">/div> before the script tag. You may also use a JavaScript library such as jQuery to ensure that the DOM is opened first before being accessed.

```html
<!DOCTYPE html>
<html>
<body>
 <div id="container"></div>
<script
src="https://ajax.googleapis.com/ajax/libs/jquery/3.3.1/jquery.min.js"></script>
<script>
document.getElementById("container").innerHTML = "Common JS Bugs and Errors";
</script>
</body>
</html>
Copy
```

17. Syntax-based

When the JavaScript programmer fails to perform a syntactically incorrect code, syntax errors occur. If the interpreter detects tokens that do not follow the basic syntax of JavaScript when creating an application, it may throw an error. According to a survey of JavaScript bug reports, such mistakes occur for 12% of all mistakes in the language.

Syntax errors in JavaScript are most often caused by grammatical errors, such as incomplete parentheses or mismatched brackets.

When using conditional statements and addressing multiple conditions, you can forget to use the parentheses, resulting in syntax errors.

Let's see the following example.

```
if((a > b) && (b < 77)

{

//more code here

}

Copy
```

Yes, the conditional statement's last parenthesis is missing. Have you seen the error in the code above?

Let's correct it.

```
if ((a > b) && (b < 77))

{

//more code here

}
```

Copy

You can spend time studying the grammatical principles of the Basic JavaScript programming language to prevent specific syntax errors. You will quickly find grammatical errors and stop shipping those with your built application if you have a lot of coding experience.

18. Undefined methods

Having a call to a function without first defining it is another important source of JavaScript bugs. According to the UBC researchers, this bug accounts for 4% of all JavaScript bugs. Here is an example:

```
var programmer = {

n: "Josh",
```

age: 26,

speak()

{

console.log(this.n);

}

};

programmer.speakNow();

Copy

On the Chrome developer console, the following error is displayed:

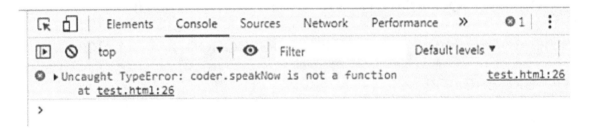

Since the called method, speakNow(), is not specified in the JavaScript code, the above error occurs.

19. Improper usage of the return statement

The return statement in JavaScript is used to stop running such that its output can be processed. When misused, the return statement will impair application results. According to the report, inappropriate use of the return expression is responsible for 2% of all JavaScript bugs.

Some JavaScript programmers, for example, often create the error of wrongly breaking the return statement.

While you can split a JavaScript statement into two lines & still get the desired result, splitting the return statement is a disaster plan. Here is an example:

```
function number(n) {

var a = 6;

return;

n + a;

}

console.log(number(11));
```

Copy

When the above code is run, an undefined error is seen on the Chrome developer console:

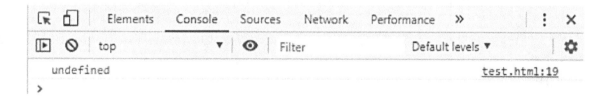

As a result, in your JavaScript code, you can avoid breaking return statements.

20. Falling in the callback hell

Callbacks are one of JavaScript's most useful features. Callbacks are no different from regular features. That is, it allows you to deal with asynchrony.

Easy callback example:

```
var results = null;
updateCustomer(customerDetails, function(data){
        results = data;
});

function updateCustomer(customerDetails, cb){
        // update customer in database
        cb(data);
}
```

As a result, the call to "updateCustomer" in the above function changes customer records in the database. You call the callback function just at the end of "updateCustomer" and transfer the result as the parameter to return the updated information.

In JavaScript, this is an easy way to handle asynchrony.

However, if not done correctly, this process of utilizing callback functions will quickly get very messy.

What happens if there are multiple functions, one of which is dependent on the output of the other?

The following is an example of how to use those functions:

```javascript
updateInfo(x, function(y){
    updateOtherInfo(y, function(z){
        updateYetOtherInfo(z, function(a){
            // ...
        });
    });
});
```

In JavaScript, the pyramid-like form above is referred to as callback hell. The long & short of it is that it is not suggested because it is difficult to follow and much more difficult to maintain.

21. Misunderstanding "===" operator

What is the difference between the operators "==" and "==="? It is a common interview question. Understanding this differentiation will help you better grasp JavaScript's quirks.

Keep it in mind to keep it simple.

"===" works in the same way as the "==" operator.

Let's look an example:

2 == "2"   // true

2 === "2" // false

In the above case, the "==" operator performed a value comparison. In other words, it implicitly modified necessary operand types and compared its equality.

However, since 2 and "2" have different data types, "===" returned false. And "===" does not convert types for you. It verifies that the operands are of the same kind and that their values are also equal.

22. Missing semicolons

JavaScript is a scripting language with a lot of intelligence. Its parsers are configured to add semicolons even when they aren't needed.

However, stay out of this vortex. It can likely backfire on you.

Look at the following example:

```
function foo(){
    return
    10
}
```

Any time the amazing "foo" function is named, it is supposed to return a value of 10. However, since JavaScript is a smart language, it interprets it in a slightly different way.

The following is JavaScript's understanding of the above function:

```
function foo(){
    return;
    10;
}
```

If you don't have semicolons, JavaScript, like the example above, can place them in unexpected places. So, to be safe put those semicolons in yourself.

23. Forgetting that variables are not block scoped

JavaScript supports function scope, one of the many variations between it and other languages, including Java and C++. It isn't a block scope.

Consider the following example to better understand function scope:

```javascript
function foo(){

    if(true){
        var y = 10;
    }

    console.log(y); // displays 10
}
```

There's an if-block in the above "foo" function. There's a variable named "y" in that if-block. It is accessing the variable "y" outside of the if-block to show its value.

Your compiler will throw an error if you attempt to do anything similar in Java or C++. It is because they are block-scoped languages. As a result, you can't access a variable outside of the code block in those languages where it's declared.

JavaScript, on the other hand, is exceptional. JavaScript supports function scope. When you attempt to enter the "y" variable outside of the if-block, it returns the value of 10.

It is due to a concept in JavaScript known as hoisting. JavaScript, in simple terms, moves all declared variables to the top of the function. As a result, those variables are accessible from anywhere in the function.

Conclusion

In this book, you'll learn about simple JavaScript concepts like arrays, variables, conditional statements, cookies, loops, and more, as well as advanced JavaScript concepts like the DOM, functional programming samples, JavaScript Unit testing systems, algorithms, and more.

There's nothing! It is a complete JavaScript beginner's guide with examples for learning JavaScript. However, having a basic understanding of CSS and HTML can help you learn more quickly and effectively.

It is for students interested in learning about web applications and software creation. This book is also beneficial for web application development professionals who want to further their experience and skills.

JavaScript is the most commonly used client-side programming language for web application creation in all industries. Candidates that are familiar with JavaScript are in high demand in the IT sector. As a result, studying JavaScript will help you land a decent job while also improving your skills and knowledge.

The design of JavaScript is determined by the environment in which it is used. Node.js, for example, has functions that enable

JavaScript to read & write arbitrary files, make network requests, and so on. JavaScript may perform various server-side (back end) and client-side (front end) roles in application development.

In-browser JavaScript often helps you manipulate webpages, interact with users, and interact with the webserver.

Following is a list of other titles we publish:

NIST SP 1800-2	Identity and Access Management for Electric Utilities
NISTIR 7628 R 1	Guidelines for Smart Grid Cybersecurity - Architecture, and High-Level Requirements
NIST SP 1800-3	Attribute Based Access Control
NIST SP 1800-6	Domain Name Systems-Based Electronic Mail Security
NIST SP 800-82	Guide to Industrial Control Systems (ICS) Security
NIST SP 1800-7	Situational Awareness for Electric Utilities
NIST SP 1800-5	IT Asset Management: Financial Services
NIST SP 500-299	NIST Cloud Computing Security Reference Architecture
NIST SP 1800-1	Securing Electronic Health Records on Mobile Devices
NIST SP 1800-4c	Mobile Device Security: Cloud and Hybrid Builds
NIST SP 800-34	Contingency Planning Guide for Federal Information Systems
NISTIR 8011	Automation Support for Security Control Assessments
DHS Study	DHS Study on Mobile Device Security
NIST SP 500-293	US Government Cloud Computing Technology Roadmap
NIST SP 800-94	Guide to Intrusion Detection and Prevention Systems (IDPS)
NIST SP 800-95	Guide to Secure Web Services
NIST SP 800-97	Establishing Wireless Robust Security Networks: A Guide to IEEE 802.11i
NIST SP 800-166	Derived PIV Application and Data Model Test Guidelines
NIST SP 800-179	Guide to Securing Apple OS X 10.10 Systems for IT Professional
NIST SP 800-191	The NIST Definition of Fog Computing
NIST SP 800-73-4	Interfaces for Personal Identity Verification
NIST SP 800-79-2	Authorization of Personal Identity Verification Card Issuers (PCI) and Derived PIV Credential Issuers (DPCI)
NISTIR 7987	Policy Machine: Features, Architecture, and Specification
NIST SP 800-53	Security and Privacy Controls for Federal Information Systems and Organizations
NIST SP 800-81-2	Secure Domain Name System (DNS) Deployment Guide
NISTIR 8074	Strategic U.S. Government Engagement in International Standardization to Achieve U.S. Objectives for Cybersecurity
NIST SP 500-291	NIST Cloud Computing Standards Roadmap
NISTIR 8011	Automation Support for Security Control Assessments
NIST SP 500-288	Specification for WS-Biometric Devices (WS-BD)
NIST SP 800-58	Security Considerations for Voice Over IP Systems
NISTIR 8055	Derived Personal Identity Verification (PIV) Credentials (DPC)

FORWARD/COMMENTARY

The National Institute of Standards and Technology (NIST) is a measurement standards laboratory, and a non-regulatory agency of the United States Department of Commerce. Its mission is to promote innovation and industrial competitiveness. Founded in 1901, as the National Bureau of Standards, NIST was formed with the mandate to provide standard weights and measures, and to serve as the national physical laboratory for the United States. With a world-class measurement and testing laboratory encompassing a wide range of areas of compute science, mathematics, statistics, and systems engineering, NIST's cybersecurity program supports its overall mission to promote U.S. innovation and industrial competitiveness by advancing measurement science, standards, and related technology through research and development in ways that enhance economic security and improve our quality of life.

The need for cybersecurity standards and best practices that address interoperability, usability and privacy has been shown to be critical for the nation. NIST's cybersecurity programs seek to enable greater development and application of practical, innovative security technologies and methodologies that enhance the country's ability to address current and future computer and information security challenges.

The cybersecurity publications produced by NIST cover a wide range of cybersecurity concepts that are carefully designed to work together to produce a holistic approach to cybersecurity primarily for government agencies and constitute the best practices used by industry. This holistic strategy to cybersecurity covers the gamut of security subjects from development of secure encryption standards for communication and storage of information while at rest to how best to recover from a cyber-attack.

Why buy a book you can download for free?   **We print this so you don't have to.**

Some are available only in electronic media. Some online docs are missing pages or barely legible.

We at 4th Watch Publishing are former government employees, so we know how government employees actually use the standards. When a new standard is released, an engineer prints it out, punches holes and puts it in a 3-ring binder. While this is not a big deal for a 5 or 10-page document, many NIST documents are over 100 pages and printing a large document is a time-consuming effort. So, an engineer that's paid $75 an hour is spending hours simply printing out the tools needed to do the job. That's time that could be better spent doing engineering. We publish these documents so engineers can focus on what they were hired to do – engineering. It's much more cost-effective to just order the latest version from Amazon.com

If there is a standard you would like published, let us know. Our web site is Cybah.webplus.net

Draft NIST Special Publication 800-71

Recommendation for Key Establishment Using Symmetric Block Ciphers

Elaine Barker
William C. Barker

C O M P U T E R   S E C U R I T Y

National Institute of
Standards and Technology
U.S. Department of Commerce

Draft NIST Special Publication 800-71

Recommendation for Key Establishment Using Symmetric Block Ciphers

Elaine Barker
Computer Security Division
Information Technology Laboratory

William C. Barker
Dakota Consulting, Inc.

June 2018

U.S. Department of Commerce
Wilbur L. Ross, Jr., Secretary

National Institute of Standards and Technology
Walter Copan, NIST Director and Under Secretary of Commerce for Standards and Technology

1
2 **Authority**
3 This publication has been developed by the National Institute of Standards and Technology (NIST) in accordance
4 with its statutory responsibilities under the Federal Information Security Modernization Act (FISMA) of 2014,
5 44 U.S.C. § 3551 *et seq.*, Public Law (P.L.) 113-283. NIST is responsible for developing information security
6 standards and guidelines, including minimum requirements for federal information systems, but such standards
7 and guidelines shall not apply to national security systems without the express approval of appropriate federal
8 officials exercising policy authority over such systems. This guideline is consistent with the requirements of the
9 Office of Management and Budget (OMB) Circular A-130.

10 Nothing in this publication should be taken to contradict the standards and guidelines made mandatory and
11 binding on federal agencies by the Secretary of Commerce under statutory authority. Nor should these guidelines
12 be interpreted as altering or superseding the existing authorities of the Secretary of Commerce, Director of the
13 OMB, or any other federal official. This publication may be used by nongovernmental organizations on a
14 voluntary basis and is not subject to copyright in the United States. Attribution would, however, be appreciated
15 by NIST.

16 National Institute of Standards and Technology Special Publication 800-71
17 Natl. Inst. Stand. Technol. Spec. Publ. 800-71, 90 pages (June 2018)
18 CODEN: NSPUE2

32
33 **Public comment period: *July 2, 2018* through *September 28, 2018***
34
35 National Institute of Standards and Technology
36 Attn: Computer Security Division, Information Technology Laboratory
37 100 Bureau Drive (Mail Stop 8930) Gaithersburg, MD 20899-8930
38 Email: SP_800-71@nist.gov
39
40 All comments are subject to release under the Freedom of Information Act (FOIA)
41

Reports on Computer Systems Technology

The Information Technology Laboratory (ITL) at the National Institute of Standards and Technology (NIST) promotes the U.S. economy and public welfare by providing technical leadership for the Nation's measurement and standards infrastructure. ITL develops tests, test methods, reference data, proof of concept implementations, and technical analyses to advance the development and productive use of information technology. ITL's responsibilities include the development of management, administrative, technical, and physical standards and guidelines for the cost-effective security and privacy of other than national security-related information in Federal information systems. The Special Publication 800-series reports on ITL's research, guidelines, and outreach efforts in information system security, and its collaborative activities with industry, government, and academic organizations.

Abstract

This recommendation addresses the protection of symmetric keying material during a key establishment that uses symmetric-key cryptography for key distribution. The objective is to provide recommendations for reducing exposure to the unauthorized disclosure of the keying material and detecting its unauthorized modification, substitution, insertion or deletion. The Recommendation also addresses recovery in the event of detectable errors during the key-distribution process. Wrapping mechanisms are specified for encrypting keys, binding key control information to the keys and protecting the integrity of this information.

Keywords

algorithm; authentication; block cipher; key distribution; key establishment; key generation; key management; key translation; key wrapping; message authentication code; symmetric key

Acknowledgements

The National Institute of Standards and Technology (NIST) gratefully acknowledges and appreciates contributions by their colleagues at NIST and the members of the ASC X9 working group that developed the standards upon which this Recommendation is based: American National Standard (ANS) X9.17, *Financial Institution Key Management (Wholesale)*, and ANS X9.28, *Financial Institution Multiple Center Key Management (Wholesale)*.

NOTE FOR REVIEWERS

This document, SP 800-71, addresses the use of symmetric block ciphers as key-establishment mechanisms.

The authors acknowledge that most current key-management systems are based on asymmetric cryptography (e.g., a Public Key Infrastructure). However, concerns associated with the projected consequences of emerging quantum computing technology for the security of existing asymmetric algorithms (see NISTIR 8105[1]) suggest a potential for some organizations to reconsider and, on a case-by-case basis, reverting to key establishment based on symmetric cryptography. Given the currently limited nature of guidance on the topic, it seems prudent to describe symmetric key-establishment techniques and security considerations.

Symmetric-key-based key establishment may also be implemented beneath an asymmetric-key-based structure to establish symmetric keys in a hierarchy after the top-most key in the hierarchy has been established using asymmetric key-establishment techniques.

Reviewers are encouraged to provide comments on any aspect of this special publication. Of particular interest are comments on the understandability and usability of the guideline. Your feedback during the public comment period is essential to the document development process and is greatly appreciated.

---

[1] *Report on Post-Quantum Cryptography.*

93

Executive Summary

95 Symmetric-key cryptography requires all originators and consumers of specific information secured
96 by symmetric functions to share a secret key. This is in contrast to asymmetric-key, or public key,
97 cryptography that requires only one party participating in a transaction to know a private key and
98 permits the other party or parties to know the corresponding public key. Symmetric-key
99 cryptography is generally much more computationally efficient than public key cryptography, so it
100 is most commonly used to protect larger volumes of information such as the confidentiality of data
101 in transit and in storage. Asymmetric cryptography is more commonly used for the establishment of
102 an initial symmetric key using key-agreement or key-transport techniques. There are circumstances
103 however, such as the discovery or emergence of serious vulnerabilities of common public key
104 algorithms to technological attacks, that may motivate individuals and organizations to use
105 symmetric-key cryptography for source authentication, data integrity and key-establishment
106 purposes.

107 This Recommendation addresses the protection of symmetric keying material during key
108 establishment using symmetric-key algorithms. The objective is to reduce the potential for
109 unauthorized disclosure of the keying material and enable the detection of unauthorized
110 modification, substitution, insertion and deletion of that keying material. The Recommendation also
111 addresses recovery in the event of detectable errors during the key-establishment process.

112 Several key-establishment architectures are described. These include:

113 • Key establishment among communicating groups that share a key-wrapping key,

114 • The distribution of keys by key generation and distribution centers to their subscribers,

115 • The use of translation centers for the protected distribution of keys generated by one subscriber
116   for distribution to one or more other subscribers, and

117 • Multiple-center-based environments for key establishment between or among organizational
118   domains.

119 The Recommendation does not specify protocols for key establishment (e.g., Kerberos, S/MIME,
120 and DSKPP). It does, however, suggest key-establishment communication options and transaction
121 content that **should** be accommodated by key-establishment protocols.

122 This Recommendation covers both the manual and automated management of symmetric keying
123 material for the federal government using symmetric-key techniques. The Recommendation
124 **should** be used in conjunction with the SP 800-57[2] series of documents and SP 800-152[3] for the
125 management of keying material, including:

126 • Control during the life of the keying material to prevent unauthorized disclosure,
127   modification or substitution;

---

[2] SP 800-57: *Recommendation for Key Management, Part 1: General, Part 2: Best Practices for Key Management,*
and Part 3: Application-Specific Key Management Guidance.
[3] SP 800-152: *A Profile for U.S. Federal Cryptographic Key Management Systems (CKMS).*

128   • Establishing communicating groups;

129   • Secure distribution of keying material to permit interoperability among communicating
130   groups;

131   • Ensuring the integrity of keying material during all phases of its life, including its
132   establishment (which includes generation and distribution), storage, entry, use, and
133   destruction;

134   • Recovery in the event of a failure of the key-establishment process or when the integrity
135   of the keying material is in question; and

136   • Auditing the key-management processes.

137   Important considerations that apply to the selection of a key-management approach include:

138   • The exposure of a key by any entity having access to that key compromises all data
139   protected by that key;

140   • The more entities that share a key, the greater the probability of exposure of that key to
141   unauthorized entities;

142   • The longer that a key is used, the greater the chance that it will become known by
143   unauthorized parties during its use;

144   • The greater the amount of data that is protected by the key, the greater the amount of data
145   that is exposed if the key is compromised;

146   • It is essential that the source of a secret or private key is trustworthy, and that a secure
147   channel be used for key distribution; and

148   • The key used to initiate a keying relationship must be obtained through a secure channel,
149   often using an out-of-band process.

150   This Recommendation provides general guidance for the establishment of symmetric keys. It is
151   intended to be a general framework within which system-specific protocols may be applied. Public
152   key cryptography is mentioned only as an alternative method for establishing an initial keying
153   relationship for a communicating group.

154

TABLE OF CONTENTS

442

1. Introduction

Symmetric-key cryptography employs cryptographic algorithms that require both the sending and receiving parties to protect communications using the same secret key. This is distinct from asymmetric-key (i.e., public key) cryptography in which the parties have pairs of keys – a private key known only to the key pair owner, and a public key that may be known by anyone. Section 3 of SP 800-175B[4] discusses the use of these two algorithm types, including the pros and cons of each, namely that:

- Symmetric-key cryptography is generally much less computationally intensive than asymmetric-key cryptography.

- Digital signatures generated using asymmetric-key algorithms provide better source authentication properties than can be provided by symmetric-key algorithms.

- The number of keys required to initiate and maintain cryptographic keying relationships is much higher for symmetric-key cryptography than for asymmetric-key cryptography.

As a result of these characteristics, recent key-management schemes have used symmetric-key cryptography for the encryption and integrity protection of data-at-rest and data-in-transit (i.e., stored or communicated data), and asymmetric-key cryptography to establish the symmetric keys for data-in-transit and for source authentication and integrity protection using digital signatures.[5]

Recent concerns associated with the projected consequences of emerging quantum-computing technology for the security of existing asymmetric algorithms (see NISTIR 8105[6]) suggest a potential federal government requirement for the reconsideration of, and possible reversion to, the use of symmetric-key cryptography. Keys protected using currently **approved** asymmetric-key algorithms[7] can, therefore, be expected to become known by adversaries once quantum computers become available. In contrast, the impact on symmetric-key algorithms will not be as drastic; doubling the size of the key will be sufficient to preserve security. Symmetric-key algorithms and hash functions with sufficiently large output should be usable in a quantum era.

Research is in progress to develop quantum-resistant asymmetric-key algorithms.[8] However, replacing the currently used asymmetric-key algorithms with quantum-resistant asymmetric-key algorithms can be expected to not really begin until about 2020 and not be completed until the 2030s.

Where the security of information is very important, and the security of information currently being protected by asymmetric-key algorithms needs to be maintained for more than a few years,

---

[4] NIST SP 800-175B, *Guideline for Using Cryptographic Standards in the Federal Government: Cryptographic Mechanisms*, August 2016.

[5] Note that symmetric key management is used in some applications such as over-the-air rekeying of digital radios. See Section 7 of SP 800-57 Part 3, *Recommendation for Key Management Part 3: Application-Specific Key Management Guidance* and Kerberos.

[6] NISTIR 8105, *Report on Post-Quantum Cryptography*, April 2016.

[7] Algorithms based on the use of difficult problems such as integer factorization, discrete logarithms, and elliptic-curve discrete-logarithms.

[8] See https://csrc.nist.gov/Projects/Post-Quantum-Cryptography.

474 moving away from the protection of symmetric keys by asymmetric-key algorithms **should** be
475 initiated as soon as practical. The protection of symmetric keys using symmetric key-wrapping
476 schemes and replacing asymmetric digital signature schemes with symmetric-key message
477 authentication schemes is one approach to replacing public key cryptographic key management in
478 the relatively near term.

479 The subject of this Recommendation is the set of security considerations associated with the use of
480 symmetric-key algorithms for key establishment. It addresses the protection of symmetric keying
481 material during key establishment to prevent unauthorized disclosure of the keying material and to
482 detect unauthorized modification, insertion and deletion. This Recommendation also addresses the
483 recovery of keys in the event of detectable errors during the key-establishment process. Several
484 high-level key-establishment strategies are presented.

485 While specific protocols (e.g., Kerberos[9], S/MIME,[10] and DSKPP[11]) are not specified in this
486 Recommendation, this document does suggest key-establishment transaction content and options
487 that **should** be accommodated by key-establishment protocols. A minimum set of requirements for
488 constructing an audit trail of the key establishment process is provided in SP 800-152.

489 Note that conformance to this Recommendation does not guarantee security. Because the
490 Recommendation is protocol-independent, the specific protocol employed for key-establishment
491 purposes needs to be analyzed for adequacy within the context of an organization's security goals.
492 Several key-establishment approaches are described in this document. Although the strategies
493 described include several key-establishment environments, the Recommendation does not
494 preclude the use of other symmetric-key management approaches.

495 1.1 Scope

496 Although this Recommendation describes the automated disribution of symmetric keying material
497 using symmetric-key techniques in automated environments, manual distribution is discussed as
498 well.

499 This Recommendation focuses primarily on strategies for the management of keys prior to their
500 use for protecting data communications. However, the Recommendation, in conjunction with the
501 SP 800-57 series of documents and SP 800-152 contain the minimum requirements for the
502 management of keying material throughout its lifecycle, including:

503 • Control during the life of the keying material to prevent unauthorized disclosure,
504   modification or substitution;

505 • Establishing communicating groups;

506 • The secure distribution of keying material to permit interoperability among communicating
507   groups;

---

[9] See Section 6 of SP 800-57 Part 3, *Recommendation for Key Management Part 3: Application-Specific Key Management Guidance.*

[10] S/MIME: Secure Multipurpose Internet Mail Extensions.

[11] DSKPP: Dynamic Symmetric Key Provisioning Protocol.

508　　　• Ensuring the integrity of keying material during all phases of its life, including its
509　　　　establishment (which includes generation and distribution), storage, entry, use, and
510　　　　destruction;

511　　　• Recovery in the event of a failure of the key-establishment process or when the integrity
512　　　　of the keying material is in question; and

513　　　• Auditing the key-management processes.

514　The scope of this document encompasses the use of only symmetric-key block-cipher algorithms
515　(e.g., FIPS 197[12]) and algorithms used to generate Message Authentication Codes (MACs) using
516　either block-cipher algorithms or using hash functions (e.g., FIPS 180-4[13] and FIPS 202[14]). The
517　use of asymmetric-key (i.e., public-key) techniques for key establishment is mentioned only as an
518　alternative method for establishing an initial keying relationship.

1.2　Content and Organization

520　The remainder of this Recommendation is organized as follows:

521　Section 2 provides definitions and common abbreviations.

522　Section 3 provides general symmetric key-management fundamentals, including uses for
523　symmetric keys, some application considerations, symmetric algorithms and key types, key-
524　distribution using symmetric-key techniques, and a discussion of key hierarchies for storage and
525　communications applications.

526　Section 4 describes general architectural considerations for the establishment of symmetric keys –
527　both center-based key establishment and key establishment among communicating groups.

528　Section 5 discusses key-establishment communications, including general communication
529　requirements, key names and key labels, message content and handling, authentication codes in
530　key-establishment messages and key revocation and destruction.

531　Appendix A contains example scenarios, and Appendix B lists document references.

---

[12] FIPS 197, *Advanced Encryption Standard (AES)*, November 26, 2001.

[13] FIPS 180-4, *Secure Hash Standard (SHS)*, March 2012.

[14] FIPS 202, *SHA-3 Standard: Permutation-Based Hash and Extendable-Output Functions*, August 4, 2015.

532 ## 2.   Definitions and Common Abbreviations

533 ## 2.1   Definitions

Acknowledgement information	Information sent to acknowledge the receipt of a communication without errors.
Advanced Encryption Standard	The encryption algorithm specified by FIPS 197, *Advanced Encryption Standard*.
Agent	See multiple-center agent.
Approved	FIPS-**approved** or NIST-recommended. An algorithm or technique that is either 1) specified in a FIPS or NIST Recommendation, or 2) specified elsewhere and adopted by reference in a FIPS or NIST Recommendation.
Asymmetric-key algorithm	A cryptographic algorithm that uses two related keys, a public key and a private key. The two keys have the property that determining the private key from the public key is computationally infeasible. Also known as a public-key algorithm.
Asymmetric-key cryptography	Cryptography that uses pairs of keys: public keys that may be widely disseminated and private keys that are authorized for use only by the owner of the key pair and known only by the owner and possibly a trusted party that generated them for the owner.
Authenticated data	Data that is accompanied by a valid message authentication code that is used to verify its source and that the data is identical to that for which the message authentication code was computed.
Authenticated encryption keys (AEKs)	Keys used to provide both confidentiality and integrity protection for the target data using the same key. Block cipher modes for using AEKs are specified in SP 800-38C[15] and SP 800-38D.[16]
Authentication	A process that provides assurance of the source and integrity of information that is communicated or stored.
Authentication algorithm	A cryptographic function that is parameterized by a symmetric key. The algorithm acts on input data (called a "message") of variable length to produce an output value of a specified length.

---

[15] SP 800-38C, *Recommendation for Block Cipher Modes of Operation: the CCM Mode for Authentication and Confidentiality.*
[16] SP 800-38D, *Recommendation for Block Cipher Modes of Operation: Galois/Counter Mode (GCM) and GMAC.*

	The output value is called the message authentication code (MAC) of the input message.
Authentication key	A symmetric key used to generate a message authentication code on a message. See Data Authentication Key (DAK).
Authenticity	The property of being genuine, verifiable and trusted; confidence in the validity of a transmission, a message, or message originator.
Automated	Using an electronic method rather than a manual method. In most cases, no human intervention is required.
Automated key establishment	The process by which cryptographic keys are securely distributed among cryptographic modules using automated methods (e.g., key transport and/or key agreement protocols).
Bi-directional (communications)	As used in this Recommendation, the same symmetric key can be used for both protecting (e.g., encrypting) sensitive data to be sent to one or more other entities and for processing (e.g., decrypting) protected data received from other entities sharing the key. Contrast with uni-directional (communications).
Block cipher	A symmetric-key cryptographic algorithm that transforms one block of information at a time using a cryptographic key. For a block cipher algorithm, the length of the input block is the same as the length of the output block.
Checksum	A value that (a) is computed by a function that is dependent on the contents of a data object and (b) is stored or transmitted together with the object, for detecting changes in the data.
Ciphertext	Data in its encrypted form.
Cloud computing facility	A facility that provides ubiquitous, convenient, on-demand network access to a shared pool of configurable computing resources (e.g., networks, servers, storage, applications, and services) that can be rapidly provisioned and released with minimal management effort or service provider interaction.
Compromise	The unauthorized disclosure, modification or use of sensitive data (e.g., keying material and other security-related information).
Confidentiality	The property that sensitive information is not disclosed to unauthorized individuals, entities, or processes.

Communicating group	Two or more logical entities that exchange data using a set of common keying material. Each communicating group has different keying material. An entity and a center participating in a key-establishment transaction do not constitute a communicating group.
Cryptographic key (Key)	A parameter used in conjunction with a cryptographic algorithm that determines its operation in such a way that an entity with knowledge of the key can reproduce or reverse the operation, while an entity without knowledge of the key cannot. Examples include: 1) The transformation from plaintext to ciphertext and vice versa for a given cryptographic algorithm, or 2) The Message Authentication Code for given data and cryptographic algorithm.
Cryptoperiod	The time span during which a specific key is authorized for use or in which the keys for a given system may remain in effect.
Data Authentication Key (DAK)	A key used for the computation of MACs in order to provide assurance of content integrity and (some level of) source authentication for cryptographically protected information.
Data Encrypting Key (DEK)	A key used for the encryption of data.
Data Key (DK)	A key used to encrypt and decrypt data, or to authenticate data.
Decryption	The process of transforming ciphertext into plaintext using a cryptographic algorithm and key.
Encryption	A process of transforming plaintext into ciphertext using a cryptographic algorithm and key.
Entity	An individual (person), organization, device, or process.
Error report information	The information in a message that reports the error that was found in a previously received message.
Hash function	A function that maps a bit string of arbitrary length to a fixed-length bit string. **Approved** hash functions satisfy the following properties: 1. (One-way) It is computationally infeasible to find any input that maps to any pre-specified output, and

	2. (Collision resistant) It is computationally infeasible to find any two distinct inputs that map to the same output.
Impact level	The magnitude of harm that can be expected to result from the consequences of unauthorized disclosure of information, unauthorized modification of information, unauthorized destruction of information, or loss of information or information system availability.
Internet Engineering Task Force (IETF)	A large, open international community of network designers, operators, vendors, and researchers concerned with the evolution of the Internet architecture and the smooth operation of the Internet.
Initialization vector (IV)	A vector used in defining the starting point of a cryptographic process.
Key	See Cryptographic key.
Key agreement	A key-establishment procedure where the resultant keying material is a function of information contributed by two or more participants, so that an entity cannot predetermine the resulting value of the keying material independently of any other entity's contribution.
Key Derivation Key (KDK)	Keys used to derive DEKs, DAKs, AEKs. and other KDKs Symmetric-key methods for key derivation are specified in SP 800-108.[17] KDKs are not used to derive KWKs.
Key Distribution Center (KDC)	Used to generate and distribute keys to entities that need to communicate with each other but may not share keys except with the center.
Key establishment	The process by which a key is securely shared between two or more entities, either by transporting a key from one entity to another (key transport) or deriving a key from information contributed by the entities (key agreement).
Key-establishment transaction	An instance of establishing secret keying material among entities. A transaction will require multiple protocol messages between two or more entities.

---

[17] SP 800-108, *Recommendation for Key Derivation Using Pseudorandom Functions.*

Key-generation request information	Information necessary to request the generation of cryptographic keys.
Key management	The activities involving the handling of cryptographic keys and other related security parameters (e.g., IVs) during the entire life cycle of the keys, including their generation, storage, establishment, entry and output, and destruction.
Keying material	The data (e.g., keys and IVs) necessary to establish and maintain cryptographic keying relationships.
Keying relationship	The state existing between entities when they share at least one symmetric key.
Key-transfer information	Information used to distribute one or more keys to a recipient.
Key Translation Center (KTC)	Used to unwrap keying material sent by one subscriber using a key-wrapping key shared with that subscriber, and to rewrap the same keying material using a different key-wrapping key shared with a different subscriber.
Key transport	A manual or automated key-establishment procedure whereby one entity (the sender) selects and distributes the key to another entity (the receiver).
Key type	As used in this Recommendation, a key categorized by its properties and uses: key-wrapping key, data authentication key, data encryption key or key-derivation key.
Key unwrapping	A method of removing the cryptographic protection on keys that was applied using a symmetric-key algorithm and key-wrapping key.
Key wrapping	A method of cryptographically protecting keys that provides both confidentiality and integrity protection for the wrapped keying material using a symmetric-key algorithm and a key-wrapping key.
Key Wrapping Key (KWK)	A key used exclusively to wrap and unwrap (e.g., encrypt, decrypt and integrity protect) other keys.
Layer 1 key	The top-most layer in a (possible) hierarchy of keys of a keying relationship.

Manual distribution	A non-automated means of transporting cryptographic keys by physically moving a device or document containing the keying material.
Master/recipient relationship	As used in this Recommendation, one (or more) members of a communicating group (i.e., masters) are allowed to generate keying material and distribute it to all other members of the group, while other members (i.e., recipients) are only allowed to receive keying material. Contrast with a peer relationship.
Message	The information transferred from one entity to another using communication protocols. This Recommendation identifies information to be included in a message but does not specify the format of that message.
Message Authentication Code (MAC)	A cryptographic checksum on data that uses a symmetric key to detect both accidental and intentional modifications of data.
Mode (of operation)	A set of rules for operating on data with a cryptographic algorithm and a key; often includes feeding all or part of the output of the algorithm back into the input of the next iteration of the algorithm, either with or without additional data being processed.
Multicast transmission	A transmission that communicates a set of information from one sender to multiple recipients simultaneously.
Multiparty control	A process that uses two or more separate entities (usually persons) operating in concert to protect sensitive functions or information. No single entity is able to access or use the materials, e.g., cryptographic keys.
Multiple-center agent	A center within a multiple-center group through which a subscriber obtains multiple-center key-establishment services.
Multiple-center group	A set of two or more centers that have agreed to work together to provide cryptographic keying services to their subscribers.
Party	Any entity, center or multiple-center agent.
Peer relationship	As used in this Recommendation, all members of a communicating group are allowed to generate or otherwise obtain keying material for distribution to the other members of the group. Contrast with a master/recipient relationship.

Protocol	A special set of rules used by two or more communicating entities that describe the message order and data structures for information exchanged between the entities.
Public key cryptography	See asymmetric-key cryptography.
Plaintext	Unencrypted (unenciphered) data.
Recipient	The entity that receives a communication.
Revocation	As used in this Recommendation, the process of permanently terminating the valid use of a key to apply cryptographic protection (e.g., wrap keying material, encrypt data or generate a MAC).
Revocation-confirmation information	Information provided to confirm that keying material has been destroyed as requested.
Revocation-request information	Information indicating the keys to be revoked and destroyed.
Secure channel	As used in this Recommendation, a path for transferring data between two entities or components that ensures confidentiality, integrity and replay protection, as well as mutual authentication between the entities or components. The secure channel may be provided using cryptographic, physical or procedural methods, or a combination thereof.
Security strength	A number associated with the amount of work (that is, the number of operations) that is required to break a cryptographic algorithm or system.
Shall	This term is used to indicate a requirement of a Federal Information Processing Standard (FIPS) or a requirement that must be fulfilled to claim conformance to this Recommendation. Note that **shall** may be coupled with **not** to become **shall not**.
Should	This term is used to indicate an important recommendation. Ignoring the recommendation could result in undesirable results. Note that **should** may be coupled with **not** to become **should not**.
Source authentication	A process that provides assurance of the source of information.
Split knowledge	A process by which a cryptographic key is split into n key components, each of which provides no knowledge of the original

	key. The components can be subsequently combined to recreate the original cryptographic key.
Subscriber	An entity that has a keying relationship with a center or agent of a multiple-center group.
Symmetric key	A single cryptographic key that is used with a symmetric-key algorithm.
Symmetric-key algorithm	A cryptographic algorithm that uses a single secret key for a cryptographic operation and its complement (e.g., encryption and decryption).
Symmetric-key cryptography	Cryptography that uses the same key for both applying cryptographic protection (e.g., encryption or computing a MAC) and removing or verifying that protection (e.g., decryption or verifying a MAC).
Target data	As used in this Recommendation, data, other than keys, that are afforded cryptographic protection.
Time-variant parameter	A time-varying value that has (at most) an acceptably small chance of repeating (where the meaning of "acceptably small" may be application specific).
Transaction	See Key-establishment transaction.
Transaction-authentication key	A key generated specifically for the key-establishment transaction that is used to generate message authentication codes for the protocol messages in that transaction.
Translation	The process performed by a center to unwrap keying material received from a sending entity (a subscriber or a center in a multiple-center group) using a key-wrapping key shared with that entity and then rewrapping the same keying material using a different key-wrapping key shared with the next recipient of the wrapped keying material (a different subscriber or a different center in the multiple-center group).
Translation-request information	Information provided to a center to request the translation of keying material contained in the request for a subscriber.
Uni-directional (communications)	As used in this Recommendation, a different symmetric key is always required for cryptographically protecting (e.g., encrypting) sensitive data to be sent to another entity than is required when processing (e.g., decrypting) cryptographically

	protected data that is received from that other entity. Contrast with bi-directional (communications).
Wrapping	See Key wrapping

534 ## 2.2   Common Abbreviations

535 This section contains abbreviations used in this Recommendation.

AEK	Authenticated Encryption Key.
AES	Advanced Encryption Standard.
DAK	Data Authentication Key.
DEK	Data Encrypting Key.
DK	Data Key.
FIPS	Federal Information Processing Standard.
KDC	Key Distribution Center.
KDK	Key Derivation Key.
KWK	Key Wrapping Key.
KTC	Key Translation Center.
MAC	Message Authentication Code.
NIST	National Institute of Standards and Technology.
NISTIR	NIST Internal or Interagency Report.
SP	Special Publication.

536

3. Symmetric-Key-Management Fundamentals

Symmetric-key algorithms (sometimes called secret-key algorithms) use a single key to both apply cryptographic protection and to remove or check the protection. For example, the key used to encrypt data (i.e., apply protection) is also used to decrypt the encrypted data (i.e., remove the protection); in the case of encryption, the original data is called the plaintext, while the encrypted form of the data is called the ciphertext. The key must be kept secret if the data is to remain protected.

The goals of symmetric-key management are 1) to provide keys and related cryptographic variables (e.g., initialization vectors (IVs)) where they are needed and 2) to keep keys secret. The security of the data protected by these keys is strictly dependent upon the prevention of unauthorized disclosure, modification, substitution, insertion, and deletion of the keys and, as appropriate, other cryptographic variables (e.g., IVs). If these are compromised, the confidentiality and integrity of the protected data can no longer be assured. General key-management guidelines are provided in SP 800-57 Part 1. Basic requirements for Key Management Systems operated by or for the Federal Government are provided in SP 800-152.

3.1 Uses of Symmetric Keys

Symmetric keys are used by block cipher algorithms (e.g., AES) that are used for encryption, key wrapping and/or the generation of message authentication codes. Symmetric keys are also used by hash function-based authentication algorithms (e.g., HMAC[18] and KMAC[19]) for the generation of message authentication codes, and for key derivation and random bit generation.

Encryption is used to provide confidentiality for data. The unprotected form of the data is called plaintext. Encryption transforms the data into ciphertext, and ciphertext can be transformed back into plaintext using decryption. Data encryption and decryption are generally provided using symmetric-key block cipher algorithms. See Section 4.1 of SP 800-175B[20] for more information regarding data encryption.

Key wrapping is a method used to provide confidentiality and integrity protection for keys (and possibly other information associated with the keys) using a symmetric key-wrapping key that is known by both the sender and receiver, and a block cipher algorithm. The wrapped keying material can then be stored or transmitted (i.e., transported) securely. Unwrapping the keying material requires the use of the same algorithm and key-wrapping key that was used during the original wrapping process. See Section 5.3.5 of SP 800-175B for more information on key wrapping.

---

[18] HMAC is specified in FIPS 198, *The Keyed-Hash Message Authentication Code (HMAC)*.
[19] KMAC is specified in SP 800-185, *SHA-3 Derived Functions: cSHAKE, KMAC, TupleHash, and ParallelHash*.
[20] SP 800-175B, *Guideline for Using Cryptographic Standards in the Federal Government: Cryptographic Mechanisms*.

568 Message authentication codes are used to protect message and data integrity. Message
569 authentication codes are cryptographic checksums on data that use symmetric-key cryptography
570 to detect both accidental and intentional modifications of data. They also provide some measure
571 of source authentication between entities sharing the same key because only entities sharing a key
572 can produce the same message authentication code. See Section 4.2 of SP 800-175B for further
573 information on message authentication codes.

574 Key derivation is concerned with the generation of a key from secret information, although non-
575 secret information may also be used in the generation process in addition to the secret information.
576 Typically, the secret information is shared among the entities that need to derive the same key for
577 subsequent interactions. The secret information could be a key that is already shared between the
578 entities (i.e., a pre-shared key), or could be a shared secret that is derived during a key-agreement
579 scheme. See Section 5.3.2 of SP 800-175B for more information regarding key derivation.

580 Cryptography and security applications make extensive use of random numbers and random bits.
581 For cryptography, random values are needed to generate cryptographic keys. There are two classes
582 of random bit generators (RBGs): Non-Deterministic Random Bit Generators (NRBGs),
583 sometimes called true random number (or bit) generators, and Deterministic Random Bit
584 Generators (DRBGs), sometimes called pseudorandom bit (or number) generators. SP 800-90A[21]
585 specifies **approved** DRBG algorithms, based on the use of hash functions and block-cipher
586 algorithms. See Section 4.4 of SP 800-175B for more information regarding random bit generation.

587 ## 3.2 Application Considerations

588 Federal agencies are required to comply with FIPS 199[22] and FIPS 200[23] in determining the
589 sensitivity of their applications and data (i.e., the target data) and the impact level associated with
590 any compromise of that data (i.e., Low, Moderate or High impact). When the impact level has been
591 determined, the security strength of the cryptographic algorithms and keys for protecting that data
592 can be determined. **PR:2.3**, **PR:2.4** and **PR:2.5** in SP 800-152 specify the minimum security
593 strengths required for the Low, Moderate and High impact levels, respectively.

594 Important considerations that apply to the selection of a key-management approach include:

595 • The exposure of a key by any entity having access to that key compromises all data
596   protected by that key;

597 • The more entities that share a key, the greater the probability of exposure of that key to
598   unauthorized entities;

---

[21] SP 800-90A, *Random Number Generation Using Deterministic Random Bit Generator Mechanisms.*
[22] FIPS 199, *Standards for Security Categorization of Federal Information and Information Systems.*
[23] FIPS 200, *Minimum Security Requirements for Federal Information and Information Systems.*

599   • The longer that a key is used, the greater the chance that it will become known by
600   unauthorized entities during its use;

601   • The greater the amount of data that is protected by the key, the greater the amount of data

> The exposure of a key by any entity having access to that key compromises all data protected by that key, and the more entities that share a key, the greater the probability of exposure of that key to unauthorized entities.

602   that is exposed if the key is compromised;

603   • It is essential that the source of a secret or private key is trustworthy, and that a secure
604   channel be used for key distribution; and

605   • The key used to initiate a keying relationship must be obtained through a secure channel,
606   often using an out-of-band process.

607   Each of these considerations must be addressed in any application of symmetric-key cryptography.

608   When using asymmetric cryptography, one entity can make one public key available to other
609   entities and use the corresponding private key in secured communications with those other entities.
610   However, when using symmetric-key cryptography, a different key is often required for each
611   correspondent. Some organizations choose to reduce this cryptographic burden by sending the
612   same symmetric key to multiple correspondents, then using that key in multicast transmissions to,
613   or exchanges with, all parties sharing that symmetric key. Drawbacks to this approach include a
614   loss of privacy and integrity protections within what are effectively cryptographic communities-
615   of-interest, and a loss of cryptographic protection by all members of the community-of-interest if
616   the shared key is compromised. There is also significant management and accounting overhead
617   associated with the distribution, installation, revocation and post-revocation access management
618   for what can be complex combinations of both distinct and overlapping cryptographic
619   communities.

620   Symmetric-key cryptography is attractive in applications that cannot afford the processing
621   overhead associated with asymmetric cryptography. This is becoming a more important factor,
622   given the rapid growth of the Internet of Things (IoT). Symmetric-key cryptography is an
623   increasingly common choice for Wireless Sensor Networks (WSN), for example, due to the limited
624   processing, storage, and electrical power available to sensors. As of 2018, asymmetric-key
625   encryption, even for key-establishment and integrity protection is impractical for many IoT sensor
626   components. An initial response to this situation has resulted in research to develop "lightweight"
627   block ciphers (see NISTIR 8114[24]) to protect sensor data and control. These "lightweight" block
628   ciphers can be defeated by current personal computers in one to a few hours (see KM in WSN).

---

[24] NIST 8114, *Report on Lightweight Cryptography.*

> The longer that a key is in use, the greater the chance that it will become known by unauthorized parties while still in use, and the greater the amount of data protected by the key, the greater the amount of data that is compromised if the key is compromised.

629 Some applications of symmetric-key cryptography reduce the initial key-management overhead
630 by establishing "crypto nets" in which many entities share the same secret key. Although there are
631 cases where operational considerations encourage the adoption of this course, the exposure of any
632 secret key tends to become more likely as the number of entities sharing the secret key increases.
633 Cyber threats, personnel security threats, physical security threats and simple carelessness on the
634 part of any entity that has access to an unencrypted secret key endangers the security of all data
635 protected by that key. This consideration argues in favor of restricting the number of entities that
636 share any given key. Exceptions that can mitigate the effects of this principle are found in isolated
637 environments, such as networks in protected facilities in which no processor that has a secret key
638 is remotely accessible.

> It is essential that the source of a secret or private key be trustworthy; the key used to initiate a keying relationship must be obtained using a secure channel.

639

640 For these reasons, keys **shall not** be used indefinitely. The period for which a key is to be used,
641 called a cryptoperiod, is established by policy based on a risk assessment. In any event, symmetric-
642 key management involves not just the initial distribution of keys, but also the distribution of
643 replacements for expired or compromised keys. Key replacement is required at a frequency
644 determined by the cryptoperiod, but emergency replacement is also required when a key in use is
645 compromised. The distribution and accounting requirements imposed by cryptoperiods and
646 emergency key replacement add significantly to key-management overheads. Note that even the
647 management of asymmetric-key pairs imposes a sufficient overhead burden that many
648 organizations seek to minimize when using cryptography. However, the key-management burden
649 is greater in the case of symmetric-key cryptography.

650 The source of any secret key has the ability to defeat any confidentiality or integrity mechanism
651 for which the key is used. Consequently, keys **shall** be accepted only from sources that can be
652 trusted with all information that is to be protected by cryptography using those keys.

653 When using asymmetric-key cryptography, a secure communications relationship can be
654 established with a new correspondent simply by making a key-establishment public key available
655 to the new correspondent. In the case of symmetric-key cryptography, a secret key must be
656 securely provided to the new correspondent. This requires either a physical transfer between
657 correspondents, a shared relationship with a center (e.g., a key distribution center) or the
658 establishment of an initial symmetric key using asymmetric key-establishment techniques.

659   Cloud-computing facilities and other large data repositories that store and/or process information
660   for physically remote customers **should** protect that information while in transit and at rest. Due
661   to its superior processing efficiency, symmetric-key cryptography is used for the encryption of the
662   information, although asymmetric-key cryptography has generally been used for key transport and
663   integrity protection and for the generation of digital signatures. Some cloud-computing facilities
664   and networks serve very large numbers of customers. Secure storage, retrieval, and general
665   management of the symmetric keys is essential to the confidentiality of customer information. It
666   also represents significant key-management overhead. Symmetric keys must never be stored or
667   transferred in unprotected form.

668   In the past, most distributions of symmetric keys involved a transfer of the keys by human couriers
669   or secure government mail systems. However, as the number of entities using a system grows, the
670   work involved in the distribution of the secret keying material could grow to be prohibitive. The
671   Internet Engineering Task Force (IETF's) provides guidelines for key management in RFC 4107[25],
672   which discusses issues associated with manual versus automated key distribution, as well as best
673   practices for key management. Consistent with RFC 4107's conclusion that, in general, automated
674   key management **should** be employed, this Recommendation focuses primarily on automated key-
675   establishment schemes. However, for any cryptographic key-management scheme that is solely
676   dependent on symmetric-key cryptography for key establishment, the initial distribution of keys
677   without the use of asymmetric-key algorithms must be manual. This is a significant cost constraint
678   and introduces architectural complexity as the size of the supported organization increases.

679   ### 3.3   Symmetric Algorithm and Key Types

680   NIST has **approved** several basic cryptographic algorithms and "modes" for using them.

681   - Block cipher algorithms (e.g., AES and TDEA[26]) that are used in specified modes to
682   perform encryption/decryption, message authentication and integrity protection, key
683   wrapping, key derivation and random bit generation.

684   - Hash functions (algorithms) that can be used to provide message authentication and
685   integrity protection, key derivation and random bit generation. The methods for providing
686   these services can be considered as hash function modes, although that term is not normally
687   used in relation to hash functions.

688   Several types of keys are used in symmetric-key cryptography.

---

[25] RFC 4107, *Guidelines for Cryptographic Key Management.*
[26] Although TDEA is currently an approved algorithm, its use is being discouraged because of security
considerations (see SP 800-131A and the NIST announcement for using TDEA).

689　　　• Key wrapping keys (KWKs) are used to wrap (i.e., encrypt and integrity protect) other
690　　　　keys, including other KWKs. KWKs are used with a block cipher algorithm as specified in
691　　　　SP 800-38F.[27]

692　　　• Data encryption keys (DEKs) are used to encrypt data other than keys (i.e., the target data).
693　　　　Block cipher modes for using DEKs are specified in SP 800-38A[28], the addendum to SP
694　　　　800-38A[29], SP 800-38E[30] and SP 800-38G.[31]

695　　　• Data authentication keys (DAKs) are used to generate message authentication codes
696　　　　(MACs) that provide integrity protection and (some measure of) source authentication for
697　　　　the target data. Block cipher modes for generating and verifying MACs are specified in SP
698　　　　800-38B[32] and SP 800-38D.[33] Hash-based techniques for generating and verifying MACs
699　　　　are specified in FIPS 198[34] and SP 800-185.

700　　　• Authenticated encryption keys (AEKs) are used to provide both confidentiality and
701　　　　integrity protection for the target data using the same key. Block cipher modes for using
702　　　　AEKs are specified in SP 800-38C[35] and SP 800-38D.

703　　　• Key Derivation Keys (KDKs) can be used to derive DEKs, DAKs, AEKs and other KDKs.
704　　　　Symmetric-key methods for key derivation are specified in SP 800-108.[36] KDKs **shall not**
705　　　　be used to derive KWKs.

706　　DEKs, DAKs and AEKs are collectively called data keys (DKs).

3.4　　Key Distribution Using Symmetric-Key Techniques

708　Keying material (i.e., keys and other cryptographic variables, such as IVs) **shall** either be
709　distributed manually (see Section 3.4.1) or using appropriate automated distribution methods (see
710　Section 3.4.2) before secure transactions begin using those keys. Keys, all other cryptographic

---

[27] SP 800-38F, *Recommendation for Block Cipher Modes of Operation: Methods for Key Wrapping.*

[28] SP 800-38A, *Recommendation for Block Cipher Modes of Operation: Methods and Techniques.*

[29] SP 800-38A Addendum, *Recommendation for Block Cipher Modes of Operation: Tree Variants of Ciphertext Stealing for CBC Mode.*

[30] SP 800-38E, *Recommendation for Block Cipher Modes of Operation: the XTS-AES Mode for Confidentiality on Storage Devices.*

[31] SP 800-38G, *Recommendation for Block Cipher Modes of Operation: Methods for Format-Preserving Encryption.*

[32] SP 800-38B, *Recommendation for the Block Cipher Mode of Operation: the CMAC Mode for Authentication.*

[33] SP 800-38D, *Recommendation for Block Cipher Modes of Operation: Galois/Counter Mode (GCM) and GMAC,* SP 800-38D.

[34] FIPS 198, *The Keyed-Hash Message Authentication Code (HMAC).*

[35] SP 800-38C, *Recommendation for Block Cipher Modes of Operation: the CCM Mode for Authentication and Confidentiality.*

[36] SP 800-108, *Recommendation for Key Derivation Using Pseudorandom Functions.*

711 variables (where needed), and accompanying documentation **shall** be protected throughout the
712 distribution process.

713 Keys **shall not** be used operationally to apply cryptographic protection (e.g., encrypt) prior to
714 sending and/or receiving acknowledgments of successful receipt or if a compromise is suspected.
715 Procedures to follow up and resolve distribution irregularities **shall** be in place (e.g., included in a
716 Key Management Practices Statement as described in SP 800-57, Part 2.[37].

717 3.4.1 Manual Distribution

718 When manual methods are used to distribute cryptographic keying material, that material **shall** be
719 distributed using couriers, registered mail, or an equivalent distribution service in which the
720 delivery agent is trusted by both the sending and receiving entities, with the recipients required to
721 identify themselves to the delivery agent and provide an appropriate receipt upon delivery. The
722 keys **shall** be transported on a medium that, together with the physical distribution method,
723 provides the required confidentiality and integrity protection for the keys.

724 Electronic media (e.g., smart cards, flash drives, or key loader devices) **should** be used during
725 manual distribution. If keys or other cryptographic variables are printed (instead of being
726 distributed using electronic media), provision **shall** be made to protect the keying material from
727 unauthorized disclosure or replacement (e.g., using uniquely identified, tamper-detecting
728 packaging). Whether using electronic media or printed material during delivery, the delivery
729 receipt **shall** identify the source of the keying material, the delivery agent, the recipient, and
730 indicate the state of the received media (e.g., no tampering detected, valid authentication codes,
731 etc.).

732 For environments where the FIPS 199 impact level associated with the data to be protected by the
733 keying material to be distributed is High, multiparty control and/or split knowledge **shall** be
734 employed when keys are distributed in plaintext form.

735 Distribution procedures **shall** ensure that:

736   (1) The distribution of keys and any other variables is authorized;

737   (2) The keying material has been received by the authorized recipient; and

738   (3) The key has not been disclosed, modified or replaced in transit.

739 The distributor (i.e., the source of the keying material) and receiver of the manually distributed
740 keys **shall** identify (to each other) those individuals who are authorized to originate, receive and
741 change keys and **shall not** reassign or delegate such responsibilities without proper notice.

---

[37] SP 800-57, Part 2: *Recommendation for Key Management: Part 2: Best Practices for Key Management
Organizations.*

3.4.2 Automated Distribution

Automated key distribution is the electronic transmission of cryptographic keys (and, where needed, other cryptographic variables such as IVs) via a communication channel (e.g., the Internet). This requires the prior distribution of an initial key-wrapping key (KWK) and an authentication key (i.e., a DAK), either manually (see Section 3.4.1) or using asymmetric key-establishment techniques (e.g., the key agreement or key transport schemes specified in SP 800-56A or SP 800-56B). The KWK and DAK may then be used to distribute all key types discussed in Section 3.3.

Keying material distributed after the initial KWK and DAK have been established **shall** be wrapped with a KWK shared between communicating entities[38] in key-establishment messages defined using a protocol that provides confidentiality, integrity protection assured delivery, and replay protection; the content of the protocol message **shall** be integrity protected using a DAK[39] (see Section 5.4). The recipient(s) **shall** unwrap the protected keys and verify their source and integrity before any cryptographic process can begin for communications using the transported key(s). If a recipient has multiple KWKs that may be used to unwrap the received keys, information **shall** be available to identify the KWK to be used (e.g., sent with the transported keying material) (see Section 5.2). Likewise, if multiple DAKs are available, a method **shall** be available to indicate the DAK used.

An SP 800-38F-compliant key-wrapping algorithm **shall** be used with a KWK for wrapping keys for automated key distribution. The key-wrapping algorithm **shall** use an **approved** symmetric encryption algorithm (i.e., AES) for wrapping one or more keys during the same key-wrapping process. Keys being wrapped may be either KWKs, KDKs, DEKs, DAKs or AEKs. The algorithm and key size used to perform the key wrapping **shall** provide security equal to or greater than the security strength to be provided to any data to be subsequently protected by the wrapped keys.

A means of protection against replay **shall** be provided in a key-establishment protocol. The use of time-variant parameters may be used to afford this protection. A nonce is a time-varying value that has (at most) an acceptably small chance of repeating (where the meaning of "acceptably small" may be application specific). See Section 5.4 of SP 800-56A or SP 800-56B for more information on nonces.

3.5 Key Hierarchies

A hierarchy of keys is often used when symmetric-key cryptography is employed for communications and storage applications.

---

[38] Either the initial KWK or a KWK subsequently distributed between the communicating entities.

[39] Either the initial DAK or a DAK subsequently distributed between entities.

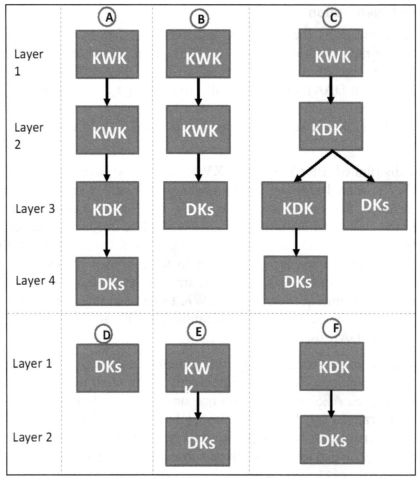

Figure 1: Examples of Symmetric-Key Hierarchies

776   Figure 1 provides several examples of symmetric-key hierarchies.

777   •   The top-most layer (Layer 1) can be any of the key types. This layer establishes a keying
778   relationship.

779   •   When the Layer 1 key is a KWK, further keys may be distributed using that KWK (see
780   examples A, B, C and E in which KWKs, KDKs, and DKs are shown at Layer 2 in the
781   figure).

782   •   A KDK at any layer has the data keys and KDKs that it derives as a lower layer (see
783   examples A, C and F).

784   •   DKs (i.e., DEKs, DAKs and AEKs) are always at the bottom of the implemented hierarchy,
785   even if the DK is a Layer 1 key, in which DKs form the only layer in the hierarchy (see
786   example D).

787   • KWKs, KDKs and DKs in a layer immediately below KWKs are wrapped by the KWK
788   above them in the hierarchy (see examples A, B, C and E).

789   The key hierarchy may not be "vertical" as shown in Figure 1 but may be somewhat more
790   horizontal; two examples are shown in Figure 2.

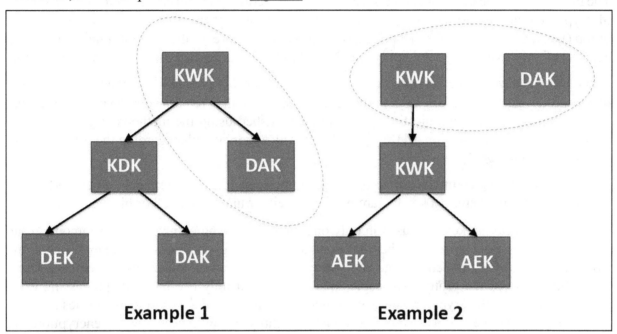

791
792   **Figure 2: Key Hierarchy Structure Examples**

793   In example 1 of the figure, the Layer 1 KWK was used to wrap a Layer 2 DAK; these keys were
794   used to establish a keying relationship (indicated in the left-hand oval). Subsequently, the KWK
795   was used to wrap a Layer 2 KDK, which was used to generate a Layer 3 DEK and DAK.

796   In example 2 of the figure, the KWK and DAK established the keying relationship (indicated in
797   the right-hand oval), but the DAK was not wrapped using the KWK as was done in the first
798   example. In this case, both the KWK and DAK are Layer 1 keys. Subsequently, the KWK was
799   used to wrap a Layer 2 KWK, which was later used to wrap two Layer 3 AEKs.

800   For the most part, the number of layers is irrelevant; the important issue is where the key is located
801   in a hierarchy, especially if the revocation of a key is required (see Section 5.5).

802   **3.5.1   Storage Applications**
803   All keys used to protect stored target data **shall** be either generated by the system in which the
804   target data is stored or generated by the sender of cryptographically protected data that is stored
805   by the recipient upon receipt. As stated in Section 3.5, the lowest layer in the key hierarchy consists
806   of the data keys (i.e., DEKs, DAKs and AEKs) used to protect the stored target data. Higher-layers

807 of keys, if used, are the KWKs used to protect the data keys or the KDKs used to derive them (see
808 Figure 1 and Figure 2).

3.5.2 Communicating Groups

810 The use of symmetric keys for communications between correspondents requires the establishment
811 of cryptographic keying relationships among two or more entities that form a communicating
812 group (i.e., a group of entities that correspond among themselves); often, a communicating group
813 consists of only two entities. An entity may be a member of more than one communicating group.

814 When using symmetric-key cryptography, a keying relationship is established when each member
815 of the group shares common keys – the Layer 1 keys of that relationship. Symmetric keying
816 relationships among communicating groups are established using the methods in Section 3.4 or
817 using key centers (see Section 4.1). Section 4.2 provides more details regarding the establishment
818 of communicating groups.

819 The keys used during communications among communicating group members (either the Layer 1
820 keys or keys below them in a key hierarchy) may be either uni-directional or bi-directional.

821 • Uni-directional keys are used in only one direction during communications among group
822   members. Each group member that is authorized to send data has its own key for applying
823   cryptographic protection (e.g., encrypting data) to be sent to other group members. Other
824   members of the group have copies of the keys, but only use them for processing (e.g.,
825   decrypting) the cryptographically protected information. For example, if Entities A and B
826   are the members of a communicating group, Entity A would use a key for encryption, but
827   Entity B would use that key only for the decrytion of information from Entity A. Entity B
828   would use a different key for encryption, and Entity A would use that same key only for
829   the decryption of information from Entity B. This approach is most appropriate for very
830   small groups (e.g., communicating pairs), or when very few group members are authorized
831   to apply protection.

832 • Bi-directional keys can be used in both directions during a communication between group
833   members; the same symmetric key is used by each member for both protecting (e.g.,
834   encrypting) sensitive data to be sent to other group members and for processing (e.g.,
835   decrypting) protected data received from other group members.

836

3.5.3 Key-Establishment Transactions

838 A key-establishment transaction is an instance of establishing keying material among or between
839 entities. This includes requests for generating keys, the generation of the keys, the distribution of
840 those keys and a confirmation of delivery. This applies to both manual and automated key
841 distribution.

842   For automated key distribution, this requires multiple protocol messages. The integrity of each
843   message and assurance of the message source is provided using a message authentication code
844   (MAC) that is generated using a transaction authentication key generated for the transaction or a
845   DAK shared between the message sender and receiver when a transaction authentication key is
846   not available (e.g., in error messages in response to messages containing the transaction
847   authentication key).

4.   Key Management Architectures for Symmetric Keys

This section describes architectural considerations for the establishment of symmetric keys and specifies architectures for different key-establishment environments. Because the security of cryptographically protected systems is largely dependent on the effectiveness of key management architectures, any such architecture must take into account organizational structures and responsibilities, and operational requirements. Key-management architecture design is best undertaken by specialists who have a comprehensive understanding of the organization, its requirements, and the risks to which it is exposed. This section describes architectural elements in general and some of the considerations associated with the design, selection, and acceptance of key management architectures.

This section provides high-level examples of key-establishment using symmetric-key systems. The general architectural approaches described include center-based key establishment and key establishment for communicating groups. Section 5 provides further information on the messages used for key establishment, and Appendix A provides more in-depth examples.

4.1   Center-based Key Establishment Architectures

Key centers can be used to mitigate one of the primary objections to the use of symmetric keys for cryptographic protections: the number of keys required to initiate and maintain cryptographic keying relationships between communicating entities (i.e., members of communicating groups) when asymmetric keys are not available for this purpose. When using key centers, each entity becomes a subscriber of a mutually trusted key center by establishing a cryptographic keying relationship with that center consisting of a KWK and a DAK. The KWK is used to wrap keying material for transport, and the DAK is used to authenticate messages when another authentication key is not available. A KWK and DAK shared between any subscribing entity and a center permits secure communications to be established between that entity and any other subscribing entity that has a KWK shared with the center.

A keying relationship between a center and its subscribers is normally established using a manual process whereby either the center or the subscriber generates the keying material and provides it to the other party. The relationship is rekeyed using the same process. Alternatively, if an asymmetric key-establishment capability is available (e.g., asymmetric key agreement or key transport), the keying material could be established using that capability. See Section 3.4.

For center-based key establishment, the center is responsible for verifying the identity of each of its subscribers, authorizing communications between subscribers by providing or not providing the services of the center, and may provide secure key-generation services.

Key center architectures have several variants: Key Distribution Centers (KDCs), Key Translation Centers (KTCs) and Multiple-Center Groups of KDCs and/or KTCs. Figure 3 depicts the keying relationships between a single center and its subscribers. The center may be either a KDC or KTC. As shown in the figure, each subscriber shares a different KWK with its center.

885

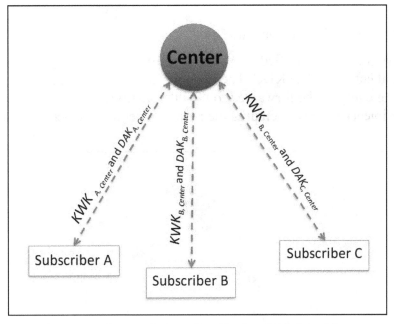

Figure 3: Center-Subscriber Keying Relationships

The keying relationship between a subscriber and a center can be used to establish keying relationships between non-center entities (e.g., subscribers A, B and C in the figure) to form communicating groups of two or more entities using automated key-establishment protocols. In cases where a KWK and DAK are established as the Layer 1 keys among subscribing entities, and at least one of those entities has key generation capabilities, subsequent key-establishment transactions may be performed without using the key center (see Section 4.2.2). The KWK and DAK that are established using the services of a key center **shall** only be replaced using the services of that center.

4.1.1   Key Distribution Centers (KDCs)

A KDC is responsible for the secure generation and distribution of keys to its subscribers, either to be used by a single subscriber for its own purposes or to be shared by multiple subscribers. KDCs may send keys either unsolicited or upon request.

When keys are intended to be shared by multiple subscribers, the KDC generates and distributes keys to subscribing entities who:

- Need to communicate with each other but either 1) do not currently share keys, 2) need to replace keys previously established using that KDC or 3) the KDC determines (of its own volition) that keys need to be shared between a subset of subscriber entities that will form a communicating group;

906   • Each share a KWK and DAK with the same KDC (i.e., each entity is a subscriber of the
907   same KDC); and

908   • May not have the ability to generate keys.

909   A copy of the keys for each identified subscribing entity is wrapped by the KDC using a KWK
910   shared between that entity and the KDC. The wrapped keys may be sent to one subscribing entity
911   (e.g., the requesting entity) to be forwarded to the other entity(ies) (see Figure 4), or may be sent
912   directly to the (recipient) entities (including the requesting entity), depending on the protocol (see
913   Figure 5).

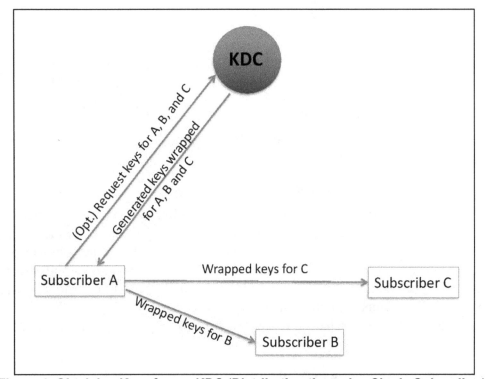

914
915   **Figure 4: Obtaining Keys from a KDC (Distributing through a Single Subscriber)**

916   Using Figure 4 as an example:

917   1) Subscriber A may optionally request that the KDC generate keying material, indicating
918   other subscribers that need to share the key (i.e., Subscribers B and C in the figure); the
919   DAK shared between Subscriber A and the KDC is used for message authentication.

920   2) Alternatively, the KDC may initiate the key distribution process without a subscriber
921   request by generating keying material to be shared by some subset of its subscribers
922   (e.g., Subscribers A, B and C in the figure).

923 3) In either case, the KDC generates the requested keying material, wraps it separately
924   using the KWK shared with each subscriber intended as a recipient. A transaction
925   authentication key (i.e., DAK) is also generated and wrapped; this DAK is in addition
926   to any other DAK included in the requested keying material.

927 4) In this example, the KDC sends all wrapped copies of the keys to Subscriber A in a
928   message that uses the transaction authentication key to generate a MAC on the outgoing
929   protocol message.

930 5) Subscriber A extracts its copy of the keys from the message and unwraps them using
931   the KWK shared with the KDC. The unwrapped transaction authentication key and the
932   received authentication code are used to check the authenticity of the message.

933 6) If the message appears to be authentic, subscriber A forwards the appropriate copy of
934   the keying material to the other intended recipient subscribers (i.e., Subscribers B and
935   C in this example) using the transaction authentication key to generate a (different)
936   MAC on each outgoing message.

937 7) Each recipient unwraps the received keying material using the KWK that is shares with
938   the KDC and uses the unwrapped transaction authentication key to check the
939   authenticity of the message.

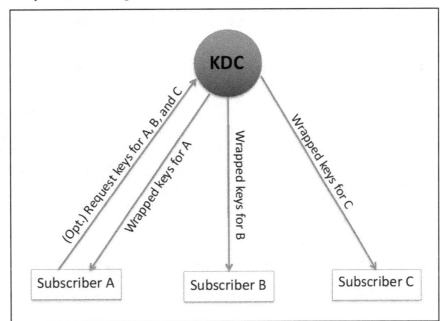

940
941   **Figure 5: Obtaining Keys from a KDC (KDC Distributes Keys to Each Subscriber Separately)**

942 Using Figure 5 as an example: steps 1, 2 and 3 are the same as the example above.

943   4) The KDC sends a message to each intended recipient (including Subscriber A) containing
944   the appropriate copy of the wrapped keying material and using the unwrapped transaction
945   authentication key to generate a (different) MAC on each outgoing message.

946   5) Each recipient unwraps the received keying material using the KWK that it shares with the
947   KDC and uses the unwrapped transaction authentication key to check the authenticity of
948   the message.

949   The scenario described in Figure 5 places more responsibility for key management overhead (e.g.,
950   accounting, revocation and suspension notice, etc.) on the KDC, while that described in Figure 4
951   places more overhead responsibility on Subscriber A. Organizational structures and assignments
952   of responsibilities can play a significant role in deciding which approach is preferable.

953   ### 4.1.2 Key Translation Centers (KTCs)

954   A Key Translation Center has the ability to translate keys for distribution to a subset of its
955   subscribers.

956   A KTC is used to translate keys for future communication between subscriber entities of the same
957   KTC who:

958   • Need to communicate with each other, but may not currently share keys;

959   • Each share a KWK and DAK with the same KTC (i.e., each entity is a subscriber of the
960   same KTC); and

961   • At least one of the subscribing entities has the ability to generate keys.

962   Keying material is generated and sent by one of the subscribers (the requesting entity) to the KTC,
963   wrapped using the KWK shared with the KTC. The KTC unwraps the keying material to be
964   translated and rewraps it using the KWK shared with other identified subscribing entity(ies) (i.e.,
965   the ultimate recipient(s)). The rewrapped keying material may be returned to the requesting entity
966   to be forwarded to the ultimate recipient(s) (see Figure 6), or may be sent directly to the ultimate
967   recipient(s), depending on the protocol (see Figure 7).

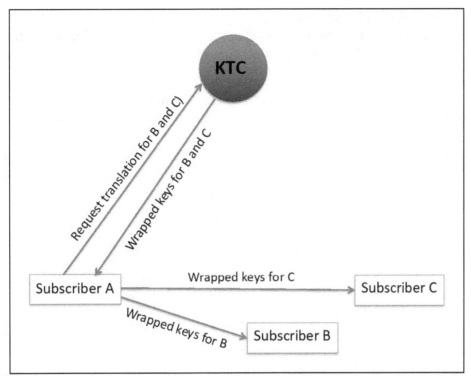

968
969 **Figure 6: Requesting Key Translation, with Keys Provided through a Single Subscriber**

970 Using Figure 6 as an example:

971 1) Subscriber A generates keying material to be shared among other KTC subscribers (i.e.,
972   Subscribers B and C in the figure); a transaction authentication key (i.e., DAK) is also
973   generated.

974 2) Subscriber A wraps the keying material (including the transaction authentication key) using
975   a KWK shared with the KTC and sends it to the KTC, indicating other subscribers that
976   need to share the keys (i.e., Subscribers B and C); the transaction authentication key is used
977   to generate a MAC on the outgoing message.

978 3) The KTC unwraps the received keying material using the KWK shared with Subscriber A
979   and uses the unwrapped transaction authentication key to check the authenticity of the
980   received message.

981 4) If the received message appears to be authentic, the KTC then rewraps the keying material
982   separately for each intended recipient using the KWK shared with that recipient.

983 5) The KTC prepares a message containing the newly wrapped keys, generates a MAC on the
984   message using the (plaintext) transaction authentication key, and sends the message to
985   Subscriber A.

30

986   6) Subscriber A forwards the appropriate copy of the keying material to the other intended
987   recipient subscribers (i.e., Subscribers B and C) using the transaction authentication key to
988   generate a (different) MAC on each outgoing message.

989   7) Each recipient unwraps the received keying material using the KWK that is shares with the
990   KTC and uses the unwrapped transaction authentication key to check the authenticity of
991   the message.

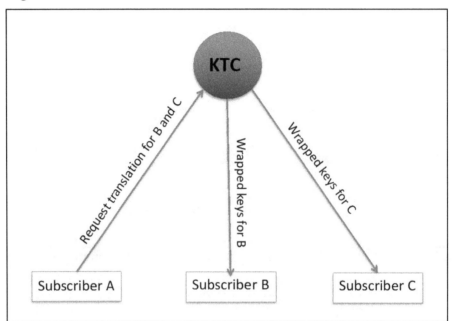

992
993   **Figure 7: Requesting Key Translation, with Keys Returned Separately to Each Subscriber**

994   Using Figure 7 as an example, steps 1 through 4 are the same as the above example.

995   5) The KTC sends a message to each intended recipient (B and C) containing the appropriate
996   copy of the wrapped keying material, using the transaction authentication key to generate
997   a (different) MAC on each outgoing message.

998   6) Each recipient unwraps the received keying material using the KWK that it shares with the
999   KTC and uses the unwrapped transaction authentication key to check the authenticity of
1000   the message.

1001   As in the case of KDCs (see Section 4.1.1), organizational structures and assignments of
1002   responsibilities can play a significant role in deciding which approach is preferable.

1003   ### 4.1.3 Multiple-Center Architectures
1004   A multiple-center group is a set of two or more centers (KDCs and/or KTCs) that have formally
1005   agreed to work together to provide cryptographic keying services to their respective subscribers. To

1006 the subscribers of a key center, the multiple-center group functions as if it were a single key center.
1007 Key centers may belong to more than one multiple-center group, but care **shall** be taken to separate
1008 domains of subscribers (e.g., subscribers for one organization from subscribers of another
1009 organization).

1010 Each center within the group has a keying relationship with at least one other center in the group:
1011 the centers share a KWK and a DAK to transport keying material between them. The centers may
1012 also distribute other keying material using their shared keys to protect messages exchanged between
1013 the centers.

1014 Every center within a multiple-center group **shall** have either a direct or an indirect keying
1015 relationship with every other center within the group (see Figure 8). Two centers have a direct
1016 keying relationship when they share a KWK and DAK (established as discussed in Section 3.4).
1017 Once the multiple-center group is established, the multiple center group **shall** use either manual or
1018 automated protocols to maintain these keying relationships (i.e., to change the shared key(s)).

1019 Two centers have an indirect keying relationship when they do not share a KWK and DAK, but there
1020 is a chain of direct keying relationships between them. In Figure 8, for example, direct keying
1021 relationships exist between Centers 1 and 2, and between Centers 2 and 3. An indirect keying
1022 relationship exists between Centers 1 and 3 because of the direct relationships that form a chain of
1023 keying relationships through Center 2.

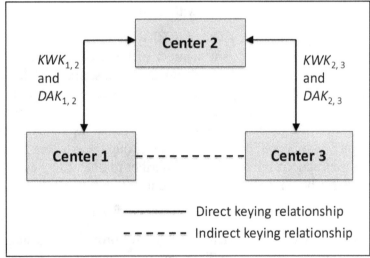

1024
1025 **Figure 8: Multiple-Center Group Direct and Indirect Keying Relationships**

1026 The use of indirect keying relationships can reduce the key management overhead associated with
1027 deploying keys among the multiple-center group members but can also reduce central control over
1028 relationships in a hierarchical environment.

1029 Centers within multiple center groups may provide key generation services. All centers within the
1030 group that have subscribers **shall** be capable of providing key translation; only a subscriber's agent

1031 (i.e., a key center to which an entity is subscribed) **shall** translate (i.e., wrap) keys for that subscriber.
1032 Some centers within the multiple-center group may only forward the keys or a request for services
1033 to the next center.

1034 Intermediate centers within the multiple center group forward information when a direct keying
1035 relationship does not exist between the agents or between an agent and a center that will generate the
1036 key(s) or perform the translation. The intermediate centers used in one portion of the information
1037 flow need not be the same as those used in another portion of the information flow. However, the
1038 number of intermediate centers used **should** be minimized.

1039 A multiple-center group **shall** be well-defined; all centers within a multiple-center group must be
1040 aware of what other centers are members of the group as well as the conditions and restrictions for
1041 group interactions. If a center belongs to more than one group, the interactions of one group **shall** be
1042 separated from the interactions of another group.

1043 The centers within a multiple-center group have specific keying relationships between them and use
1044 communication protocols to manage those keying relationships[40] and fulfill requests from their
1045 subscribers.

1046 Multiple-center groups can be used to support the establishment of keying relationships between
1047 subscribers of different centers that belong to the multiple-center group (e.g., to establish
1048 communicating groups). Depending on the group design, every subscriber of a center within the
1049 group may or may not be able to establish keys with all subscribers of all centers within the group.

1050 Each subscribing entity associated with a KDC or KTC within a multiple-center group has a keying
1051 relationship with at least one center that is a member of the group; this center is the subscriber's
1052 "agent" for the group; however, a center need not have subscribers of its own. Entities (i.e.,
1053 subscribers) may have more than one agent for a multiple-center group, and a subscriber may
1054 subscribe to more than one multiple-center group using the same or a different agent. Using a center
1055 as an agent to a group does not preclude using the same center as a single-center KDC or KTC.
1056 Interaction with the other members of a multiple-center group by an agent is a service provided by
1057 that agent center. Key transactions initiated by a subscriber to one of its agents **shall** be fulfilled or
1058 acknowledged to the subscriber through that same agent.

1059 The following services may be provided to the subscribers by a multiple-center group.

1060 • A key-distribution service is equivalent to the service provided by a single-center KDC. One
1061 or more centers within the group **shall** be capable of generating keying material; however,
1062 only one center (i.e., only one KDC) within the multiple-center group **shall** generate the
1063 keying material for a single key-distribution process. Key generation may be in response to
1064 a request from a subscriber to its agent (one of the centers within the multiple-center group)
1065 or as determined by a center within the group. Agent centers within the multiple-center group

---

[40] This is similar in concept to the use of cross certification between PKI Certification Authorities.

are responsible for wrapping the key(s) intended for their subscriber(s) under KWKs shared with those subscribers. All copies of the wrapped keys may be sent to a single subscriber for forwarding to the other intended recipients or provided to each recipient subscriber by its multiple-center agent.

- A key-translation service is equivalent to the service provided by a single-center KTC. KTCs forward copies of the key to the appropriate center(s) within the group for each subscriber designated to receive a copy of the key. All copies of the wrapped keys may be sent to a single subscriber or provided to the subscribers by their respective multiple-center agent.

The following subsections provide high-level examples of interactions between subscribers and their agent centers and between centers within the multiple-center group. In these examples, all keying material is sent directly to the intended recipient(s). However, the keying material could also be returned to one subscriber, who distributes it to other subscribers. The examples do not address error handling; this is included in the more-detailed examples in Appendices A.5 and A.6.

4.1.3.1　A Subscriber Requests Key Generation and Distribution Services

In this example, a subscriber of an agent center requests key-generation services for keying material to be subsequently shared among a list of entities that are subscribers of some agent within the multiple-center group; this process starts at step 1) below. Alternatively, a center within the group could initiate the process for a predetermined list of entities (starting at step 2a or 3a).

1) A subscriber (i.e., the requesting subscriber) sends a key-generation request to its agent center, indicating the other intended recipients of the keying material. A MAC is generated on the outgoing message using the DAK shared with the agent.

2) If the agent can generate the requested keying material:

    a) The agent generates the requested keying material and a transaction authentication key, wraps a copy of the keys (including the transaction authentication key) for the requesting subscriber using the KWK shared with that subscriber, and sends them to the subscriber, using the transaction authentication key to generate a MAC on the outgoing message.

    b) For each intended recipient that is a subscriber of that agent: The agent wraps a copy of the keys using the KWK shared with each intended recipient and sends them to that subscriber, using the transaction authentication key to generate a MAC on the outgoing message. Alternatively, these copies could be sent in the same message as those intended for the requesting subscriber (see step 2a).

    c) For each intended recipient that is not a subscriber of that agent:

        - The agent attempts to determine a path through the multiple-center group to that recipient's agent for translation of the keys to be sent to that recipient.

- The keying material is wrapped using a KWK shared with the next center in the path for transport to that center. A separate transaction authentication key is generated for multiple-center group communications, wrapped using the KWK shared with the next center in the path, and used to generate a MAC on the outgoing message.

d) If a center receives a translation request from another center within the multiple center group, and that center is not the agent for the intended recipient (i.e., the center is an intermediate center):

- The receiving center unwraps the received keying material using the KWK shared with the previous center and uses the unwrapped group transaction authentication key to check the authenticity of the received message.

- If the received message appears to be authentic, the center then attempts to determine a path to the intended recipient's agent and wraps the keying material (including the group transaction authentication key) using a KWK shared with the next center in the path for transport to that center.

- A MAC is generated on the outgoing message using the unwrapped group transaction authentication key.

e) If a center receives a translation request from another center within the multiple center group, and the receiving center is the agent for the intended recipient:

- The agent center unwraps the received keying material using the KWK shared with the previous center and uses the unwrapped group transaction authentication key to check the authenticity of the received message.

- If the received message appears to be authentic, the agent center wraps the keying material to be translated (including the transaction authentication key, but not the group transaction authentication key) and sends it to the intended recipient, using the transaction authentication key to generate a MAC on the outgoing message.

f) Any subscriber receiving wrapped keying material unwraps it using the KWK shared with its agent and uses the unwrapped transaction authentication key to check the authenticity of the received message.

3) If the agent center or another center within the group receives a request to generate keying material but is unable to do so:

a) The center checks the authenticity of the received message using the DAK shared with the subscriber or center having sent the generation request.

The center then forwards the request to a center within the group that can generate the requested keying material. Intermediate centers may be required. The forwarded request uses the DAK shared with the next center to generate a MAC on the outgoing message.

b) When a center with a key-generation capability (a key-generation center) receives the request:

- The authenticity of the received message is checked using the DAK shared with the subscriber or center that sent or forwarded the generation request.
- The requested keying material is generated, as well as a transaction authentication key.
- Keying material destined for any subscriber of that center is wrapped using a KWK shared with that subscriber and sent to that subscriber, using the transaction authentication key to generate a MAC on the outgoing message.
- For any intended recipient that is not a subscriber of the key-generation center, go to step 2c above, proceeding through steps 2 d, e and f, as appropriate.

4.1.3.2   A Subscriber Requests Key-Translation Services

In this example, a subscriber of an agent center generates keying material and requests translation services for keying material to be subsequently shared among a list of entities that are subscribers of some agent within the multiple-center group.

1) A subscriber generates keying material (including a transaction authentication key), wraps the keys using a KWK shared with its agent center and sends a translation request to the agent, indicating the intended recipients. The transaction authentication key is used to generate a MAC on the outgoing message.

2) When an agent center receives a translation request:

- The center unwraps the keying material using the KWK shared with the requesting subscriber and checks the authenticity of the received request using the unwrapped transaction authentication key.

- If any intended recipient is also a subscriber of that agent center, the agent wraps the keying material (including the transaction authentication key) using a KWK shared with that recipient and sends it to the recipient, using the transaction authentication key to generate a MAC on the outgoing message.

- For any intended recipient that is not a subscriber of that agent:

  - The agent attempts to determine a path through the multiple-center group to that recipient's agent for translation of the keying material.

  - If the agent is capable of generating keys, a group transaction authentication key is generated.

  - The keying material is wrapped (including the newly generated group transaction authentication key, if available) using a KWK shared with the next center in the path for transport in a translation request to that center. A MAC is generated on the

1170   outgoing message using the newly generated group transaction authentication key
1171   (if available) or using the transaction authentication key sent in the translation key
1172   if not; an indication of which key is used must be present (referred to as the
1173   "appropriate authentication key" below).

1174   3) If a center receives a translation request from another center within the multiple center group,
1175   and that center is not the agent for the intended recipient (i.e., the center is an intermediate
1176   center):

1177   • The receiving center unwraps the received keying material using the KWK shared with
1178   the previous center and checks the authenticity of the received message using the
1179   "appropriate authentication key."

1180   • The center then attempts to determine a path to the intended recipient's agent and wraps
1181   the keying material (including the "appropriate authentication key") using a KWK shared
1182   with the next center in the path for transport to that center.

1183   • A MAC is generated on the outgoing message using the "appropriate authentication
1184   key."

1185   4) If a center receives a translation request from another center within the multiple center
1186   group, and that center is the agent of the intended recipient:

1187   • The agent center unwraps the received keying material using the KWK shared with
1188   the previous center and uses the unwrapped "appropriate authentication key" to check
1189   the authenticity of the received message.

1190   • The agent center wraps the keying material to be translated (including the transaction
1191   authentication key, but not the group transaction authentication key, if present) and
1192   sends it to the intended recipient, using the transaction authentication key to generate
1193   a MAC on the outgoing message.

1194   5) Any subscriber receiving wrapped keying material unwraps it using the KWK shared with
1195   its agent and uses the unwrapped transaction authentication key to check the authenticity of
1196   the received message.

4.2   Communicating Groups

1197

1198 This section discusses the establishment of a communicating group and the subsequent distribution
1199 of additional keying material within that group. Also see Section 3.5.2.

4.2.1   Establishing Communicating Groups

1200

1201 Communicating groups of two or more entities share keys for communication among the group
1202 members. Prior to or during the establishment of a communicating group, each prospective
1203 member of the group **shall** have assurance of the validity of the group, the source and method of

group establishment, the identity of the other group members and the rules for group operation (e.g., using contracts, security policies, memoranda of agreement).

The Layer 1 keys that establish the keying relationship among the group members **shall** be established using one of the following methods:

a) Manual distribution as discussed in Section 3.4.1,

b) Use key centers or multiple-center groups: Each member of a prospective communicating group would become a subscriber of the same key center or of an agent center of the same multiple-center group (see Section 3.4 and Section 4.1).

- One member of the intended group requests the generation of a key for distribution to the other intended members of the group from a KDC or multiple center group (see Sections 4.1.1 and 4.1.3),

- A KDC or multiple-center group (of its own volition) generates a key and sends it to the intended group members (see Sections 4.1.1 and 4.1.3),

- One member of the intended communicating group generates a key and sends it to a KTC for translation for the intended members of the group (see Section 4.1.2), or

c) The key is established using asymmetric key-establishment methods. Each member of a prospective communicating group could obtain an asymmetric key-establishment key pair and the associated public key certificate. The entity generating the Layer 1 keys could then use the public key associated with each group member to distribute the Layer 1 keys to that member.

4.2.2 Communicating Group Requirements

1) A key used by any communicating group **shall** not intentionally be used by any other communicating group.

2) When replacing a Layer 1 key (e.g., at the end of its cryptoperiod or because of a compromise), the key **shall** be replaced in the same manner as it was established.

3) A key shared among a communicating group **shall** not be disclosed to a different communicating group. If a member of a communicating group is also a member of another group, that member **shall not** use or disclose that key to other members of the other group. For example, if entity A is a member of both group 1 and group 2, a key used in group 1 **shall not** be either used or disclosed to other members of group 2 unless they are also members of group 1.

4) A key shared among a communicating group **shall** be secured from third entity usage, except for an entity that was involved in the distribution of that key (e.g., a key center, see Section 4.1).

5) A key that has been used by a communicating group or other cryptographic keying relationship and revoked **shall** not be intentionally re-used for any subsequent interaction (also see Section 5.5).

4.2.3 Subsequent Key Distribution within a Communicating Group

Once a communicating group is established (see Section 4.2.1), the members can operate as peers or in master/recipient relationships for subsequent key-distribution operations. A peer relationship exists when all members of the group are allowed to generate or otherwise obtain (e.g., using a KDC) keying material for distribution to the other members of the group. In a master/recipient relationship, one (or more) members of the group (i.e., masters) are allowed to generate keying material and distribute it to all other members of the group, while other members (i.e., recipients) are only allowed to receive keying material.

Note that keys can only be distributed using automated methods if the group shares a KWK.

When the group shares a KDK (e.g., examples A, C and F in Figure 1), some member (or pre-established rule) needs to decide when to derive a new data key or KDK from the already-shared KDK.

If a communicating group shares a KWK (e.g., examples A, B, C and E in Figure 1), and at least one member of the group has a key generation capability, then additional keys may be generated and distributed within the group without the assistance of key centers. The member entity that generates the key wraps the newly generated key under a KWK shared with the other members of the group (the recipients); the recipients unwrap the received key using the same shared KWK.

5.   Key-Establishment Communications

This section addresses key-establishment communication requirements for communicating groups; communications between KDCs, KTCs and multiple-center groups and their subscribers; and communications among the member centers in a multiple-center group.

5.1 General Communications Requirements

Automated symmetric-key establishment is dependent on communications among components of the key-management infrastructure. Communications in support of key establishment **should** be accomplished according to system-wide protocols. The protocols **shall** establish the key-establishment information content to be used for the automated establishment of keying material.

Although this Recommendation does not specify key-management protocols, some general guidelines are offered regarding processing rules to be followed in key establishment.

a) All key-establishment messages **shall** have integrity and source authentication protection using an **approved** message authentication algorithm (e.g., HMAC or KMAC) and a secret DAK shared between the sender and receiver.

b) When a key-generation capability is available, a newly generated authentication key **should** be generated for an outgoing message containing keys if a KWK is available for wrapping the authentication key.

c) Messages carrying keys **shall** include the key(s) used to authenticate the message, protected by a shared KWK or a KWK sent in the message.

d) Before taking action on received key-establishment messages, the receiving entity **shall**:

- Attempt to verify the authentication code in the received message (see Section 5.4). If an error is detected, an error message **shall** be sent to the message sender.

- Check the authenticity/validity/authorizations/reasonableness of other information carried in the received message (e.g., using nonces or sender IDs). If an error is detected, an error message **shall** be sent to the message sender.

- If another message is not to be immediately sent to the message sender in response to a request, an acknowledgement message **shall** be sent to the message sender.

e) Messages sent in response to messages carrying keys **should** use the authentication key sent in the previous message for computing the authentication code on the responding message. However, if the authentication code in the received message could not be verified, another authentication key shared by the message sender and receiver **shall** be used for computing the message authentication code on the responding error message.

f) In order to facilitate secure key establishment, keys may need to be uniquely identified by key names or labels. The assignment of a label to a key **shall** be made only by the entity or center that generates the key or requests the generation of a key with a specified label. Once a key is labeled, the label **shall** not be changed.

Keys may be uniquely identified by:

(1) The sharing entities,

(2) A key identifier (i.e., key name),

(3) The key type (e.g., KWK or DEK),

(4) The key subtype (i.e., manually or electronically distributed KWK, authentication or encryption data key) and/or

(5) The effective date of the key[41].

The sharing entities and key type of a key carried in a key-establishment message or used to wrap a key carried in a key-establishment message **should** be specified in that message.

5.2 Notation

In Section 5.3 and the examples in Appendix A, information sets to be included in protocol messages are formatted as follows:

> *information_name*(*parameter_set_1*; *parameter_set 2* {; ...; *parameter_set_n*}),

where each parameter set has one or more items separated by commas.

Keys and variable information in a parameter set is italicized; other information is not.

Keys are indicated by the type of key (e.g., KWK), subscripted by the identities of the sharing entities or the name of the key, e.g., $KWK_{A, B}$ or DAK_{name}.

Keys are wrapped as follows:

> *wrapped_keys* = WRAP(*wrapping_key, concatenation_of_keys_to_be_wrapped*).

5.3 Message Content and Handling

This section recommends information that **should** be included in key-establishment messages and provides guidance in handling them when received. The section identifies information that needs to be included in each type of message, but not the format to be employed or other information to be included in a specific protocol message.

Key-establishment messages are used to:

- Request the generation or translation of keying material,

- Acknowledge the receipt of a request for key generation or translation services,

- Provide keying material to other entities,

- Acknowledge the receipt of keying material,

- Request the revocation of keys,

- Confirm that keys have been destroyed in response to a revocation request, and

- Report errors in key-establishment messages, providing information that may allow error recovery.

---

[41] The effective date could be the begin date, the end date, or the cryptoperiod.

1327 Additional message types may be required by a particular key-management infrastructure.

1328 The following key-establishment information sets are recommended for incorporation into
1329 protocol messages. Specific protocols may combine the functionality of two or more sets of
1330 recommended information into a single protocol message when appropriate. Similarly, a protocol
1331 may employ more than one protocol message to convey the information identified for each
1332 information set listed below. The specification of the actual messages to be used in a
1333 communication protocol **should** be carefully designed to fulfill the participant's policy
1334 requirements for secure communications.

1335 Examples for using these information types are provided in Appendix A.

5.3.1 Key Generation Request

1337 A *key generation request* permits entities within a key-management infrastructure to request that
1338 keys be generated. The request may be sent:

1339 • By one member of a communicating group (entity B) to another member of that group
1340 (entity A),

1341 • From one entity (B) to another entity (A) to request the services of a KDC, KTC or
1342 multiple-center group (e.g., to establish a communicating group),

1343 • By a KDC subscriber (A) to a KDC or a multiple-center group, or

1344 • By a center within a multiple-center group (Center 1) to another center within the group
1345 (Center 2) who may or may not have a key-generation capability.

1346 The request may be transitive (e.g., from Subscriber B through Subscriber A to a KDC), and the
1347 request may be forwarded until it is received by an entity that is capable of servicing the request
1348 (e.g., from B to A to Center 1 to Center 2) or until it is determined that the service is not available.

1349 A *key-generation request* **shall** indicate the types of keying material to be generated
1350 (*requested_keys*) and the intended communicating group [42] for using those keys. The
1351 *requested_keys* information might include the key types (e.g., KWK and DAK), the algorithm
1352 (e.g., AES), the key length (e.g., 256 bits) and a label for each key, or other information, as
1353 appropriate.

1354 The request **shall** provide for the authentication of the requesting entity and for integrity protection
1355 of the message containing the *key-generation request* information using an authentication key
1356 (*auth_key*) to generate an authentication code (*auth_code*) on the message (see Section 5.4):

1357 **key-generation_request**(*requested_keys*; *communicating_group*; *auth_code*).

1358 See example scenarios in Appendices A.1, A.2, A.3 and A.5 for the use of *key-generation request*
1359 information. Appendix A.1 discusses the distribution of a key in a communicating group (i.e., the
1360 group members already share a KWK and DAK). Appendix A.2 discusses the distribution of keys
1361 using a KDC; Appendix A.3 discusses the establishment of a communicating group using a KDC;
1362 and Appendix A.5 discusses the establishment of a communicating group using a multiple-center
1363 group to generate and distribute keys to the communicating group.

---

[42] This could, for example, be a list of entity IDs or a number assigned to a communicating group.

5.3.2 Key Transfers

Keying material is transferred from one entity (i.e., the sender) to one or more other entities (i.e., the receiver(s)). The keying material is sent as *key transfer* information from a KDC, KTC or agent of a multiple-center group to one of its subscribers, or from one member of a communicating group to one or more other members of that group.

Keying material transported in a message containing *key transfer* information **shall** be wrapped using a KWK shared between the sender and the intended receiver. Keying material to be transported in the *key transfer* information **shall** be cryptographically protected as follows:

Let $KWK_{S, R}$ be a KWK shared between the *key transfer* information sender (S) and the *key transfer* information receiver (R).

If one or more KWKs are included in the *key transfer* information:

- At least one KWK **shall** be wrapped using $KWK_{S, R}$.

- Other KWKs **shall** be wrapped using either $KWK_{S, R}$ or another KWK included in the *key transfer* information, with an indication of the specific KWK that was used.

If one or more KDKs or DKs (i.e., DEKs, DAKs, or AEKs) are included in the *key transfer* information:

- If no KWKs are included in the *key transfer* information, then the KDK(s) and/or DKs **shall** be wrapped using $KWK_{S, R}$

- If KWKs are included in the *key transfer* information, the KDK(s) and/or DK(s) **shall** be wrapped using either $KWK_{S, R}$ or a KWK included in the *key transfer* information, with an indication of the specific KWK that was used.

Key transfer information **shall** include the wrapped keying material (*wrapped_keys*), an indication of the communicating group members, and provide integrity protection for the entire message and authentication of the entity sending the keying material using an authentication key (*auth_key*) that is included with the wrapped keys and used to generate an authentication code (*auth_code*) that is generated on the message (see Section 5.4):

$$\textbf{\textit{key\_transfer}}(\textit{wrapped\_keys};\ \textit{communicating\_group};\ \textit{auth\_code}).$$

Appendix A provides multiple examples of using *key transfer* information in various scenarios.

5.3.3 Translation Requests

A *translation request* transfers keying material from one entity to a second entity for translation of that keying material for delivery to a third entity. Use cases include the following:

a) The first entity is a KTC subscriber, who generates keys and sends the *translation request* to a KTC (the second entity), who is being requested to translate the keying material for another KTC subscriber (the third entity). An example is provided in Appendix A.4.

b) The first entity is a subscriber of a center that serves as an agent to a multiple-center group (the second entity). The group is being requested to translate the keying material for a third entity, who is presumed to be a subscriber of some center within the multiple-center group. An example is provided in Appendix A.6.

c) The sender of the *translation request* is a center within a multiple-center group, and the receiver is another center within the group. The request may need to be forwarded until a center is found that can perform the requested translation for the ultimate recipient of the keying material (the third party, a subscriber of some center within the multiple-center group). Examples are provided in Appendices A.5 and A.6.

In order to send *translation request* information, the sending entity **shall** share a KWK with the receiver of the

translation request (e.g., a KTC or agent center within a multiple-center group). In order to fulfill the request, a KTC or another center within the multiple-center group **shall** share a KWK with the intended ultimate recipient of the keying material.

A message containing *translation request* information **shall** include wrapped keying material (*wrapped_keys*) and indicate who requested the translation (*requester*) and the communicating group that will use the keying material. Integrity protection **shall** be provided using an authentication key (*auth_key*) generated for each message containing *translation request* information for computing an authentication code (*auth_code*) on the message (see Section 5.4).

> **translation_request**(*wrapped_keys*; *requester*; *communicating group*; *auth_code*).

5.3.4 Revocation Request

Revocation request information is used to request the destruction of the operational and backup copies of keying material. Keys may be revoked by any entity authorized to do so (e.g., authorized in an organization's security policy; by agreement among communicating group; or in an agreement with a KDC, KTC or multiple-center group). The *revocation request* and corresponding *revocation confirmation* information (see Section 5.3.5) may be forwarded if required.

The *revocation request* information **shall** identify the keying material to be destroyed (*key_list*) and provide for the authentication and authorization of the entity requesting the destruction (*requester*) and the integrity of the message using an authentication code (*auth_code*) that is generated using an authentication key (*auth_key*). The authentication key **shall** be newly generated for the message containing the *revocation request* information if the sender can generate keys, and the sender (*S*) and receiver (*R*) share a KWK ($KWK_{S, R}$). Otherwise, the authentication key **shall** be a key already shared by the sender and receiver.

In either case, the authentication key (*auth_key*) **shall** be used to compute an authentication code (*auth_code*) on the message (see Section 5.4):

(1) If a newly generated authentication key is used, then:

> **revocation_request**(*key_list*; *requester*; *wrapped_auth_key*; *auth_code*),

where *wrapped_auth_key* = WRAP($KWK_{S, R}$, *auth_key*).

(2) If the sender cannot generate keys, or a KWK is not shared between the sender and receiver:

> **revocation_request**(*key_list*; *requester*; *auth_key_ID*; *auth_code*),

where *auth_key_ID* is used to identify the key used to compute the authentication code (*auth_code*).

1441 Any keys shared between the sender and the receiver(s) may be revoked. If a key at a given layer
1442 is revoked, all keys below it in the key hierarchy **shall** be revoked. For example, if a keying
1443 relationship was established by a KWK, and the KWK was used later to wrap a KDK, then the
1444 revocation of that KDK also revokes all data keys and other KDKs derived from that KDK.

1445 Note that if all Layer 1 keys shared with the receiver(s) are revoked, the relationship among the
1446 sender and those receivers is terminated.

1447 Archived copies of a revoked key may be retained if stored in a secure archive facility.

1448 Examples of using revocation requests are provided in Appendix A.8.

5.3.5 Revocation Confirmation

1450 A message containing *revocation confirmation* information provides notification that keys were
1451 destroyed as requested in previously received *revocation request* information. The *revocation*
1452 *confirmation* information **shall** indicate the message containing the *revocation request* information
1453 to which it is responding (*revocation_request_id*) and provide for the authentication of the entity
1454 sending the confirmation and a method of detecting the integrity of the message containing the
1455 *revocation confirmation* information using an authentication code (*auth_code*) computed using the
1456 authentication key used for the message containing the *revocation request* information. An
1457 indication of the key(s) that were destroyed (*list_of_revoked_keys*) **shall** also be included if this
1458 can be accomplished without introducing security weaknesses:

1459   ***revocation_confirmation**(revocation_request_id; list_of_revoked_keys; auth_code)*.

1460 Examples of using revocation confirmations in response to revocation requests are provided in
1461 Appendix A.8.

5.3.6 Acknowledgements

1463 An acknowledgement is used to report the receipt of a message without communication errors or
1464 other reasons for not acting upon the received message. An acknowledgement is appropriate when:

1465 a) A message containing *key-generation request* information is received, but the request is
1466   forwarded to another entity (e.g., a KDC or multiple-center group); in this case, the
1467   recipient of the *key-generation request* information cannot generate the requested keying
1468   material.

1469 b) A message containing *key tran*sfer information has been received correctly;

1470 c) A message containing *translation request* information is received, but the request is
1471   forwarded to another entity.

1472 A message containing *acknowledgement* information **shall** indicate the communication being
1473 acknowledged (*previous_message_id*) and provide for the authentication of the entity sending the
1474 message and a method of detecting its integrity using a previously established authentication key
1475 (*auth_key*) to generate an authentication code (*auth_code*) (see Section 5.4):

1476   ***acknowledgement**(previous_msg_id; auth_code)*.

1477 1. If the *acknowledgement* information is sent in response to a message containing *key-*
1478   *generation request* information, the sender (of the *acknowledgement* information)

presumably does not have a key-generation capability (otherwise, a newly generated key would be returned). In this case, an authentication key **shall** use a previously established key for the purpose.

2. If the *acknowledgement* is sent in response to messages containing *key transfer* or *translation request* information, the authentication code **shall** be generated using the authentication key (*auth_key*) used for the message being acknowledged.

Multiple examples of the use of messages containing *acknowledgement* information are provided in Appendix A.

5.3.7   Error Reports

An error message is used to report an error in the previously received key-establishment message. The error message is used to notify the sender of the previous message that the receiver could not act on the previous message information because of an error (e.g., the authentication code for the received message could not be verified, or the request cannot be fulfilled).

The *error report* information in the message **shall** indicate the previous message that is in error, provide for the authentication of the entity sending the error message and a method of detecting its integrity using a previously established authentication key (*auth_key*) to compute an authentication code (*auth_code*) on the message (see Section 5.4). An indication of the specific error (*error_type*) **shall** also be provided if this can be accomplished without introducing weaknesses in the protocol:

$$error\_report(previous\_message\_id; error\_type; auth\_code).$$

Multiple examples of the use of messages containing *error report* information are provided in Appendix A.

5.4   Authentication Codes in Key-Establishment Messages

As required in Section 5.1, an authentication code is required on all key-establishment messages. The authentication code is generated on the entire message (with the exception of the authentication code itself) using an **approved** authentication algorithm and the authentication key (*auth_key*). The authentication algorithm may be indicated in the key-establishment message, negotiated between the sender and receiver or determined by the communications protocol.

The authentication key may have been previously established between the sender and receiver (e.g., manually or in a previous message) or may be carried in the message itself (e.g., in a message containing *key transfer* or *translation request* information). If carried in a message, the sender (of the outgoing message) **shall** wrap the authentication key using a KWK either contained in the message or already shared between the sender and receiver; a receiver must unwrap the key in order to verify the authentication code in the message.

The authentication code **shall** be verified by a receiver before taking action on the key-establishment information in any received message (see Section 5.1).

- If the verification fails, a message containing *error report* information **shall** be sent to the message sender (see Section 5.3.7).

- If the verification is successful and another message is not to be immediately sent to the message sender in response to a request, an acknowledgement **shall** be sent to the message sender (see Section 5.3.6).

5.5   Revocation and Destruction

General guidance regarding the destruction of cryptographic keys is provided in SP 800-57 Part 1 and in SP 800-88. Except for archival purposes, when keys have been compromised, suspected of having been compromised, or revoked, they **shall** be physically or logically destroyed so that they cannot be recovered (e.g., by overwriting with another key or a constant value).

For a keying relationship (e.g., between members of a communicating group or between a center and a subscriber), if a key is revoked, all keys that are lower in that key's hierarchy **shall** be revoked. For example, if a Layer 1 KWK shared by a communicating group is used to protect a KDK distributed within the group, a revocation of the KDK requires the destruction of that KDK and all data keys and other KDKs derived from that KDK; a revocation of the Layer 1 KWK requires the destruction of the KWK and all keys below it in the key hierarchy. If a Layer 1 key is revoked, and there is no other Layer 1 key to continue a keying relationship (e.g., for a communicating group), then the relationship **shall** be terminated.

Cryptographic keys **shall** be destroyed in accordance with SP 800-88. FIPS140 contains suggested methods for the destruction of keying materials within cryptographic modules.

- The destruction of keys **shall** be accomplished under conditions of full accountability, with appropriate records retained for audit trail purposes. Note that some keys (e.g., derived keys, and some other locally generated one-time or short-term keys) are not usually recorded and may be exempt from accounting rules. See SP 800-57, Part 2, for accounting guidelines for cryptographic keys.

Appendix A: Example Scenarios

This appendix contains examples using the key-establishment information specified in <u>Section 5</u> in various scenarios.

Note that error handling of received acknowledgements is often suggested, but is not included in detail.

A.1   Communicating Group Key Transfer

In this example, a communicating group was established between two entities as discussed in <u>Section 4.2</u>. As shown in <u>Figure A.1</u>, Entities A and B share a KWK to be used for key wrapping, and a DAK to be used for authentication when needed (i.e., $KWK_{A,B}$ and $DAK_{A,B}$); these two keys are the Layer 1 keys shared by the group. In this example, Entity A can generate keys, but Entity B cannot.

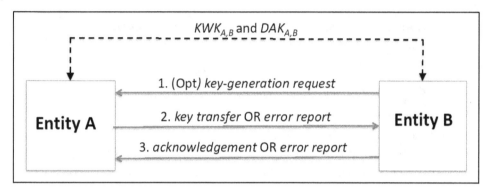

Figure A.1: Key-Generation Request and Key Transfer in a Communicating Group

1. If Entity B would like to exchange information with Entity A, then Entity B could, for example, send a *key-generation request* to Entity A asking for an AEK to be used with the AES-128 block cipher:

    key-generation_request(AEK: AES-128; *communicating group*: Entity_A, Entity_B; $auth\_code_1$).

    where $auth\_code_1$ is generated using the shared DAK ($DAK_{A,B}$).

2. Entity A generates keys in response to requests from Entity B or of its own volition.

    (a) If Entity A receives a *key-generation request*: Entity A attempts to verify that the message containing the *key-generation request* (see step 1) was correctly received from a member of the communicating group (i.e., Entity B). If the verification fails, then an error message is sent to Entity B containing *error report* information, and further interaction is terminated.

    error_report(*previous_message_id*; *error_type*; $auth\_code_2$),

    where *previous_message_id* is the ID for the *key-generation_request* (see step 1), the *error_type* is the type of error, and $auth\_code_2$ is generated using $DAK_{A,B}$.

    Entity B could choose to resend the *key-generation request* (see step 1).

    (b) When Entity A generates a key for Entity B (either in response to a verified request from Entity B or of its own volition), a transaction authentication key is also generated ($Transaction\_DAK_{A,B}$) rather than using the already-shared authentication key (i.e., $DAK_{A,B}$). Entity A wraps the key to be sent (K) and the transaction authentication key using the shared KWK ($KWK_{A,B}$):

$$wrapped\_keys = \text{WRAP}(KWK_{A,B}, K \parallel Transaction\_DAK_{A,B}).$$

    (c) The *wrapped_key* is sent to Entity B in a message containing *key transfer* information:

key_transfer(*wrapped_keys*; *communicating_group*: Entity_A, Entity_B; *auth_code₃*),

where *auth_code₃* is generated using $Transaction\_DAK_{A,B}$.

3. When the *key transfer* information is received, Entity B sends either an *acknowledgement* or an *error report*.

    (a) Entity B unwraps the wrapped keys and uses $Transaction\_DAK_{A,B}$ to attempt a verification of the message. If the verification fails, an error message is sent to Entity A containing *error report* information:

error_report(*previous_message_id*; *error_type*; *auth_code₄*),

where *previous_message_id* is the ID for the message containing the *key transfer* information (see step 2c), the *error_type* is the type of error, and *auth_code₄* is generated using $DAK_{A,\,B}$. Since the message had an error, $Transaction\_DAK_{A,\,B}$ may not have been received correctly, so $DAK_{A,\,B}$ is used as the authentication key.

Entity A may resend the *key transfer* information (see step 2c).

    (b) If the verification of the authentication code is successful, a message containing *acknowledgment* information is sent:

acknowledgement(*previous_msg_id*; *auth_code₅*),

where *previous_message_id* is the ID for the message containing the *key transfer* information (see step 2c), and *auth_code₅* is generated using $Transaction\_DAK_{A,\,B}$.

Note that for the sake of brevity, Entity A's receipt and handling of the *acknowledgement* information is not discussed in detail here. However, if the message containing the *acknowledgement* information cannot be verified, then Entity A could send an error message to Entity B, and Entity B could resend the *acknowledgement* information (see step 3b).

A.2 Using a KDC to Distribute Keys to an Already-Established Communicating Group

Entities A and B are members of a communicating group; they share $KWK_{A,\,B}$ and $DAK_{A,\,B}$ as their Layer 1 keys. Neither entity can generate keying material. However, they are subscribers of the same KDC.

Entity A shares $KWK_{A,\,KDC}$ and $DAK_{A,\,KDC}$ with the KDC; Entity B shares $KWK_{B,\,KDC}$ and $DAK_{B,\,KDC}$ with the KDC. Additional keying material can be generated by the KDC and distributed to A

1606　and B. Figure A.2a and Figure A.2b depict two alternatives, differing only in how the keys are
1607　distributed to A and B after generation by the KDC.

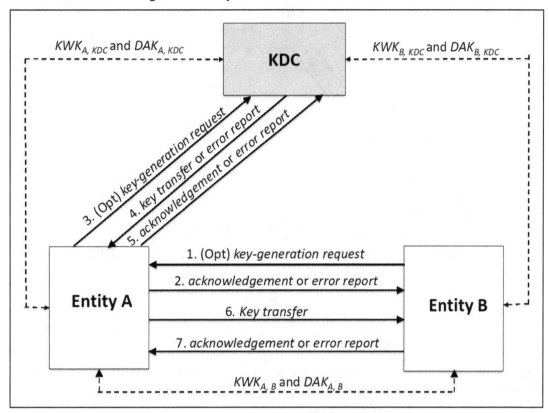

1608
1609　**Figure A.2a: Using a KDC (Alternative 1)**

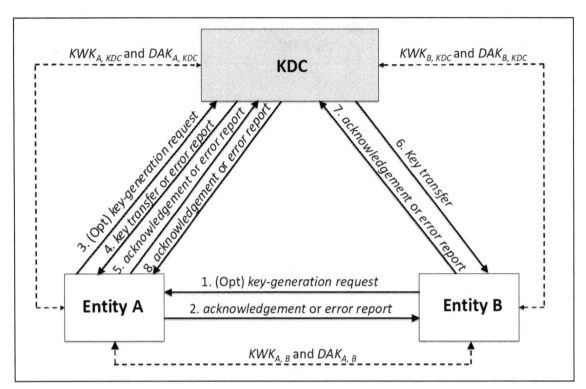

1610

Figure A.2b: Using a KDC (Alternative 2)

1612　1.　Entity B may optionally send a *key-generation request* to Entity A asking for a KWK to be
1613　　　used with the AES-128 block cipher.

1614　　　　　***key-generation_request***(KWK: AES-128; *communicating_group*: Entity_A, Entity_B;
1615　　　　　　　　　　　　　　　　　　　　　　*auth_code₁*).

1616　　　where *auth_code₁* is generated using the shared DAK ($DAK_{A,B}$).

1617　2.　(a) If Entity A receives a *key-generation request* (see step 1): Entity A attempts to verify that
1618　　　　　the message containing the *key-generation request* was correctly received from a member
1619　　　　　of the communicating group (i.e., Entity B).　If the verification fails, then an error message
1620　　　　　is sent to Entity B containing *error report* information, and further interaction is
1621　　　　　terminated.

1622　　　　　　　　***error_report***(*previous_message_id*; *error_type*; *auth_code₂*),

1623　　　　where *previous_message_id* is the ID for the message containing the *key-*
1624　　　　*generation_request* (see step 1), the *error_type* is the type of error, and *auth_code₂* is
1625　　　　generated using $DAK_{A,B}$.

1626　　　　Entity B could choose to resend the *key-generation request* (see step 1).

1627　　　(b) If the verification of the authentication code is successful, a message containing
1628　　　　　*acknowledgment* information is sent to Entity B:

1629　　　　　　　　***acknowledgement***(*previous_msg_id; auth_code₃*),

1630　　　　where *previous_message_id* is the ID for the message containing the *key-generation*
1631　　　　*request* (see step 1) and *auth_code₃* is generated using $DAK_{A,B}$.

3. Entity A sends a *key-generation request* to the KDC asking for a KWK to be used with the AES-128 block cipher and shared with Entity B:

$$\textbf{\textit{key-generation\_request}}(\text{KWK: AES-128; } \textit{communicating\_group: } \text{Entity\_A, Entity\_B;}$$
$$\textit{auth\_code}_4),$$

where *auth_code*$_4$ is generated on the message containing the *key-generation request* using the DAK shared with the KDC ($DAK_{A, KDC}$).

4. (a) The KDC attempts to verify *auth_code*$_4$ using the DAK shared with Entity A ($DAK_{A, KDC}$). If the verification fails or if Entity B is not a subscriber of the KDC, *error report* information is returned to Entity A in an error message, and the process is terminated.

$$\textbf{\textit{error\_report}}(\textit{previous\_message\_id; error\_type; auth\_code}_5),$$

where *previous_message_id* is the ID for the message containing the *key-generation request* (see step 3), *error_type* is the type of error, and *auth_code*$_5$ is generated using $DAK_{A, KDC}$.

If the error was because of a verification failure, Entity A may choose to resend the *key-generation request* (see step 3). If a *key-generation request* was received from Entity B (see step 1), Entity A may notify Entity B of the problem in an error message (not shown in the figures).

(b) If the verification of the *key-generation_request* is successful, and Entity B is a subscriber of the KDC, the KDC generates the requested key (K) and an authentication key (*Transaction_auth_key*), and wraps one copy of the keys using the KWK shared with Entity A ($KWK_{A, KDC}$) and another copy of the keys using the KWK shared with Entity B ($KWK_{B, KDC}$).

$$\textit{Entity\_A\_wrapped\_keys} = \text{WRAP}(KWK_{A, KDC}, K \parallel \textit{Transaction\_auth\_key})$$

$$\textit{Entity\_B\_wrapped\_keys} = \text{WRAP}(KWK_{B, KDC}, K \parallel \textit{Transaction\_auth\_key}).$$

At this point in the process, go to Alternative 1 or Alternative 2.

Alternative 1 (using Figure A.2a): Continuing at step 4 (c).

(c) The two copies of the wrapped keys are sent to Entity A in a *key transfer* message:

$$\textbf{\textit{key\_transfer}}(\textit{Entity\_A\_wrapped\_keys, Entity\_B\_wrapped\_keys;}$$
$$\textit{communicating\_group: } \text{Entity\_A, Entity\_B; } \textit{auth\_code}_6),$$

where *auth_code*$_6$ is generated using *Transaction_auth_key*.

5. (a) Upon receiving the *key_transfer* information, Entity A extracts its copy of the wrapped keys from the message (see step 4c), unwraps the keys using the KWK shared with the KDC ($KWK_{A, KDC}$), and checks the message's authentication code (*auth_code*$_6$) using the unwrapped transaction authentication key (*Transaction_auth_key*).

(b) If the verification of the authentication code fails, then an error-report message is sent to the KDC containing *error_report* information:

$$\textbf{\textit{error\_report}}(\textit{previous\_message\_id; error\_type; auth\_code}_7),$$

where *previous_message_id* is the ID for the message containing the *key_transfer* information (see step 4c), the *error_type* is the type of error, and *auth_code$_7$* is generated using $DAK_{A,\ KDC}$. Note that since there was an error in the received message, the wrapped authentication key (*Transaction_auth_key*) in the message may not be correct, so $DAK_{A,\ KDC}$ is used as the authentication key.

The KDC may choose to resend the *key_transfer* information (see step 4c).

(c) If the verification of the authentication code is successful, a message containing *acknowledgment* information is sent to the KDC:

$$\textbf{\textit{acknowledgement}}(\textit{previous\_msg\_id};\ \textit{auth\_code}_8),$$

where *previous_message_id* is the ID for the message containing the *key transfer* information (see step 4c), and *auth_code$_8$* is generated using *Transaction_auth_key*.

6. Entity A creates and sends a message to Entity B containing *key transfer* information that includes Entity B's copy of the wrapped keys:

$$\textbf{\textit{key\_transfer}}(\textit{Entity\_B\_wrapped\_keys};\ \textit{communicating\_group}:\ \text{Entity\_A, Entity\_B};\ \textit{auth\_code}_9),$$

where *auth_code$_9$* is computed on the message using the transaction authentication key received from the KDC (*Transaction_auth_key*).

7. Entity B sends either *acknowledgement* or *error_report* information to Entity A after receiving the message.

(a) Entity B extracts the wrapped keys from the received *key transfer* information (see step 6), unwraps the keys using the KWK shared with the KDC ($KWK_{B,\ KDC}$), and checks the message's authentication code (*auth_code$_9$*) using the unwrapped authentication key (*Transaction_auth_key*).

(b) If the verification of the authentication code fails, then an error message is sent to Entity A containing *error report* information.

$$\textbf{\textit{error\_report}}(\textit{previous\_message\_id};\ \textit{error\_type};\ \textit{auth\_code}_{10}),$$

where *previous_message_id* is the ID for the message containing the *key transfer* information (see step 6), the *error_type* is the type of error, and *auth_code$_{10}$* is computed on the message using $DAK_{A,\ B}$. Since the received message had an error, *Transaction_auth_key* may have been received incorrectly, so $DAK_{A,\ B}$ is used as the authentication key.

Entity A may resend the *key transfer* message (see step 6).

(c) If the verification of the authentication code is successful, then a message containing *acknowledgement* information is sent to Entity A:

$$\textbf{\textit{acknowledgement}}(\textit{previous\_msg\_id};\ \textit{auth\_code}_{11}),$$

where *previous_message_id* is the ID for the message containing the *key transfer* information (see step 6), and *auth_code$_{11}$* is generated using *Transaction_auth_key*.

Note that for the sake of brevity, Entity B's receipt and handling of the *acknowledgement* information is not discussed in detail here. However, if the message containing the

1707
1708
1709

acknowledgement information cannot be verified, then Entity B could send an error message to Entity A, and Entity A could resend the *acknowledgement* information (see step 7c).

1710   At this point, both Entity A and Entity B know that they have successfully received the new KWK.

1711   **Alternative 2** (using Figure A.2b): Continuing at step 4 (c).

1712
1713

(c) The KDC sends a message containing *key transfer* information to Entity A with the appropriate copy of the wrapped keys:

1714
1715

key_transfer(*Entity_A_wrapped_keys*; *communicating_group*: Entity_A, Entity_B; *auth_code*$_{12}$),

1716   where *auth_code*$_{12}$ is generated using *Transaction_auth_key*.

1717
1718
1719
1720

5. (a) Entity A extracts the wrapped keys from the received message (see step 4c), unwraps the keys using the KWK shared with the KDC (*KWK*$_{A, KDC}$), and checks the message's authentication code (*auth_code*$_{12}$) using the unwrapped authentication key (*Transaction_auth_key*).

1721
1722

(b) If the verification of the authentication code fails, then an error message containing *error report* information is sent to the KDC.

1723   **error_report**(*previous_message_id*; *error_type*; *auth_code*$_{14}$),

1724
1725
1726
1727
1728

where *previous_message_id* is the ID for the message containing the *key transfer* information (see step 4c), the *error_type* is the type of error, and *auth_code*$_{14}$ is generated using *DAK*$_{A, KDC}$. Note that since there was an error in the received message, the wrapped authentication key (*Transaction_auth_key*) in the message may not be correct, so *DAK*$_{A, KDC}$ is used as the authentication key.

1729   The KDC may resend the message containing the *key transfer* information (see step 4c).

1730
1731

(c) If the verification of the authentication code is successful, then a message containing *acknowledgement* information is sent to the KDC.

1732   **acknowledgement**(*previous_msg_id*; *auth_code*$_{15}$),

1733
1734

where *previous_message_id* is the ID for the message containing the *key transfer* information (see step 4c), and *auth_code*$_{15}$ is generated using *Transaction_auth_key*.

1735
1736
1737

6. If the KDC receives an acknowledgement from Entity A (indicating that Entity A has the keying material), the KDC sends a message containing *key transfer* information to Entity B with the appropriate copy of the wrapped keys:

1738
1739

key_transfer(*Entity_B_wrapped_keys*; *communicating_group*: Entity_A, Entity_B; *auth_code*$_{13}$),

1740   where *auth_code*$_{13}$ is generated using *Transaction_auth_key*.

1741
1742
1743
1744

7. (a) Entity B extracts the wrapped keys from the *key transfer* information in the received message (see step 4c), unwraps the keys using the KWK shared with the KDC (*KWK*$_{B, KDC}$), and checks the message's authentication code (*auth_code*$_{13}$) using the unwrapped authentication key (*Transaction_auth_key*).

(b) If the verification of the authentication code fails, then an error message is sent to the KDC containing *error report* information.

$$\boldsymbol{error\_report}(previous\_message\_id;\ error\_type;\ auth\_code_{16}),$$

where *previous_message_id* is the ID for the message containing the *key transfer* information (see step 4c), the *error_type* is the type of error, and *auth_code$_{16}$* is generated using *DAK$_{B, KDC}$*. Note that since there was an error in the received message, the wrapped authentication key (*Transaction_auth_key*) in the *key transfer* information may not be correct, so *DAK$_{B, KDC}$* is used as the authentication key.

The KDC may resend the message (see step 4c).

(c) If the verification of the authentication code is successful, then a message containing *acknowledgement* information is sent to the KDC.

$$\boldsymbol{acknowledgement}(previous\_msg\_id;\ auth\_code_{17}),$$

where *previous_message_id* is the ID for the message containing the *key transfer* information (see step 4c), and *auth_code$_{17}$* is generated using *Transaction_auth_key*.

Note that for the sake of brevity, the KDC's receipt and handling of the *acknowledgement* information is not discussed in detail here. However, if the message containing the *acknowledgement* information cannot be verified, then the KDC could send an error message to Entity B, and Entity B could resend the *acknowledgement* information (see step 7c).

8. At this point, the KDC and Entity B know that Entities A and B share the new keys (because of the protocol flow; see steps 5 and 6), but Entity A has has not been notified of this fact.

The KDC sends an a message to Entity A containing acknowledgement information indicating that Entity B has successfully received the new keys:

$$\boldsymbol{acknowledgement}(previous\_msg\_id;\ auth\_code_{18}),$$

where *previous_message_id* is the ID for the message containing the *key generation request* (see step 3), and *auth_code$_{18}$* is generated using *Transaction_auth_key*.

Note that for the sake of brevity, Entity A's receipt and handling of the *acknowledgement* information is not discussed in detail here. However, if the message containing the *acknowledgement* information cannot be verified, then Entity A could send an error message to the KDC, and the KDC could resend the *acknowledgement* information (see step 7c).

If the acknowledgement message is successfully verified, Entities A and B now know that they share the new keys.

A.3   Using a KDC to Establish a Communicating Group

Entities A and B do not share keys, but a decision has been made that they need to communicate securely. This can be done using the services of a KDC to form a communicating group.

Both entities share keys with the same KDC. Entity A shares *KWK$_{A, KDC}$* and *DAK$_{A, KDC}$* with the KDC; Entity B shares *KWK$_{B, KDC}$* and *DAK$_{B, KDC}$* with the KDC (see Figure A.3).

In this example, Entity A (the requesting subscriber) requests the KDC to generate keys to be shared with Entity B in order to form a communicating group. The KDC generates the requested keys and sends them to Entity B. After receiving an acknowledgement from Entity B that the keys have been received correctly, the KDC sends the keys to Entity A. When an acknowledgement of correct receipt has been received from Entity A, the communicating group is considered to be established.

Variants of this scenario are possible but would require other message flows. For example, when the KDC begins the process by sending keys to a subset of subscribers without receiving a request, one or more additional messages may be required to provide assurance to the entities that they do indeed share keys and form a communicating group (e.g., messages from the KDC or between the entities). If communicating groups are larger than two entities, then additional messages will be required to distribute the keys to the additional entities and to provide mutual assurance that the group has been completely established.

The steps following Figure A.3 discuss the case where one subscriber (Entity A) requests the KDC to generate keys for Entity B.

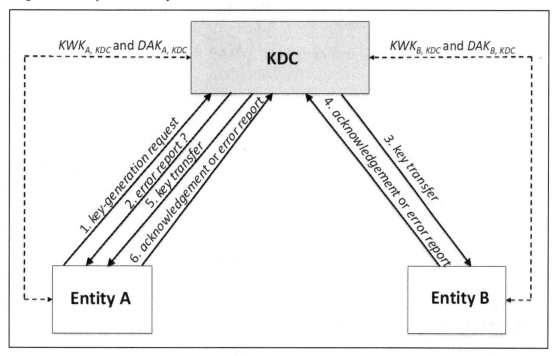

Figure A.3: Establishing a Communicating Group Using a KDC

1. Entity A sends a *key-generation request* to the KDC asking for a KWK and DAK to share with Entity B:

$$\textbf{\textit{key-generation\_request}}(KWK, DAK; \textit{communicating\_group}: \text{Entity\_A, Entity\_B}; \textit{auth\_code}_1),$$

where *auth_code*$_1$ is generated on the message containing the *key-generation request* using the DAK shared with the KDC ($DAK_{A, KDC}$).

2. The KDC attempts to verify that the message containing the *key-generation request* was correctly received and that Entity B is a KDC subscriber. If the verification fails, then an error message is sent to Entity A containing *error report* information, and further interaction is terminated.

$$\textbf{\textit{error\_report}}(\textit{previous\_message\_id}; \textit{error\_type}; \textit{auth\_code}_2),$$

where *previous_message_id* is the ID for the message containing the *key-generation_request* (see step 1), the *error_type* is the type of error, and *auth_code*$_2$ is generated using $DAK_{A,\,KDC}$.

Entity A could choose to resend the *key-generation request* (see step 1).

3. (a) The KDC generates the requested keying material to be shared between Entities A and B ($KWK_{A,\,B}$ and $DAK_{A,\,B}$) and a transaction authentication key (*Transaction_auth_key*). In this example, $KWK_{A,\,B}$ is intended to be a Layer 1 key, with $DAK_{A,\,B}$ beneath it in the key hierarchy. This will allow a termination of the communicating group in the future by revoking just the Layer 1 key (see Section 5.5 and Appendix A.8, Example 1). Therefore, $KWK_{A,\,B}$ is wrapped using the KWK shared with the intended receiving entity (A or B), and $DAK_{A,\,B}$ is wrapped using $KWK_{A,\,B}$. For efficiency reasons, the transaction authentication key is wrapped using the KWK shared with the intended receiving entity:

$$Entity\_A\_wrapped\_KWK\_and\,auth\_key = \text{WRAP}(KWK_{A,\,KDC}, KWK_{A,\,B}\,\|$$
$$Transaction\_auth\_key);$$

$$Entity\_B\_wrapped\_KWK\_and\,auth\_key = \text{WRAP}(KWK_{B,\,KDC}, KWK_{A,\,B}\,\|$$
$$Transaction\_auth\_key);$$

$$wrapped\_DAK = \text{WRAP}(KWK_{A,\,B}, DAK_{A,\,B}).$$

(b) The KDC creates and sends a message containing *key transfer* information to Entity B (see step 3a):

$$\textbf{\textit{key\_transfer}}(Entity\_B\_wrapped\_KWK\_and\,auth\_key, wrapped\_DAK;$$
$$communicating\_group: \text{Entity\_A, Entity\_B}; auth\_code_3),$$

where *auth_code*$_3$ are generated using *Transaction_auth_key*.

4. (a) Entity B extracts and unwraps $KWK_{A,\,B}$ and *Transaction_auth_key* using the KWK shared with the KDC ($KWK_{B,\,KDC}$), and checks the message's authentication code (*auth_code*$_3$) using the unwrapped authentication key (*Transaction_auth_key*).

(b) If the verification of the authentication code fails, or if Entity B does not wish to establish a communicating group with Entity A, then an error message is sent to the KDC containing *error report* information.

$$\textbf{\textit{error\_report}}(\textit{previous\_message\_id}; \textit{error\_type}; \textit{auth\_code}_4),$$

where *previous_message_id* is the ID for the message containing the *key transfer* information (see step 3b), the *error_type* is the type of error, and *auth_code*$_4$ is generated using $DAK_{B,\,KDC}$. Note that when there is an error in the received message, the wrapped authentication key (*Transaction_auth_key*) in the *key transfer* information may not be correct, so $DAK_{B,\,KDC}$ is used as the authentication key. Also, if Entity B does not want to establish a communicating group with Entity A, using the authentication key received in the *key transfer* information (*Transaction_auth_key*) may not be desirable.

The KDC may resend the *key transfer* message (see step 3b). Alternatively, the KDC may send *error report* information to Entity A indicating that the keys could not be established with Entity B (not shown in the figure).

(c) If the verification of the authentication code is successful, and Entity B wants to establish a communicating group with Entity A, then Entity B unwraps $DAK_{A, B}$ using $KWK_{A, B}$.

(d) Entity B sends a message to the KDC containing *acknowledgement* information:

$$\textbf{\textit{acknowledgement}}(previous\_msg\_id; auth\_code_5),$$

where *previous_message_id* is the ID for the message containing the *key transfer* information (see step 3c), and *auth_code*$_5$ is generated using *Transaction_auth_key*.

5. Upon receiving a message from Entity B containing the *acknowledgement* information and verifying its correct receipt (left as an exercise for the reader!), the KDC prepares and sends key transfer information to Entity A:

$$\textbf{\textit{key\_transfer}}(Entity\_A\_wrapped\_keys; communicating\_group: Entity\_A, Entity\_B;$$
$$auth\_code_6),$$

where *auth_code*$_6$ are generated using *Transaction_auth_key*.

6. (a) Entity A extracts the wrapped keys from the received message (see step 5), unwraps the keys using the KWK shared with the KDC ($KWK_{A, KDC}$), and checks the message's authentication code (*auth_code*$_6$) using the unwrapped authentication key (*Transaction_auth_key*).

(b) If the verification of the authentication code fails, then an error message containing *error report* information is sent to the KDC.

$$\textbf{\textit{error\_report}}(previous\_message\_id; error\_type; auth\_code_7),$$

where *previous_message_id* is the ID for the message containing the *key transfer* information (see step 5), the *error_type* is the type of error, and *auth_code*$_7$ is generated using $DAK_{A, KDC}$. Note that since there was an error in the received message, the wrapped authentication key (*Transaction_auth_key*) in the message may not be correct, so $DAK_{A, KDC}$ is used as the authentication key.

The KDC may resend the message containing the *key transfer* information (see step 5).

(c) If the verification of the authentication code is successful, then a message containing *acknowledgement* information is sent to the KDC.

$$\textbf{\textit{acknowledgement}}(previous\_msg\_id; auth\_code_8),$$

where *previous_message_id* is the ID for the message containing the *key transfer* information (see step 5), and *auth_code*$_8$ is generated using *Transaction_auth_key*.

At this point, Entities A and B share a KWK and DAK as members of the same communicating group. However, only Entity A knows for sure that the keys are shared (because of the order that

1880   the keys were distributed by the KDC in this example). Entity B could be notified of this fact in a
1881   couple of ways:

1882   • By Entity A or B sending a cryptographically protected message to the other party (e.g.,
1883   protected using the newly established KWK and DAK); or

1884   • By the KDC sending acknowledgement information to Entity B indicating that the
1885   establishment of the communicating group has been completed.

A.4   Using a KTC to Establish a Communicating Group

1886

1887   Entities A and B do not share keys, but a decision has been made that they need to communicate
1888   securely. This can be done using the services of a KTC to form a communicating group.

1889   In this example, Entity A generates Layer 1 keys to be shared with Entity B and sends them to the
1890   KTC for translation. The KTC translates the keys and sends them to Entity B. After receiving an
1891   acknowledgement that the keys have been received correctly by Entity B, the KTC sends an
1892   acknowledgement of correct receipt to Entity A; the communicating group is then considered to
1893   be established.

1894   Variants of this scenario are possible but would require other message flows. For example, if
1895   communicating groups are larger than two entities, then additional messages will be required to
1896   distribute the keys to the additional entities and to provide mutual assurance that the group has
1897   been completely established.

1898   Figure A.4 shows the use of a KTC by two entities (A and B) that want to establish a
1899   communicating group. Both entities are subscribers of the same KTC; Entity A shares $KWK_{A, KTC}$
1900   and $DAK_{A, KTC}$ with the KTC; Entity B shares $KWK_{B, KTC}$ and $DAK_{B, KTC}$ with the KTC. In this case,
1901   Entity A can generate keying material. For this example, the KTC does not generate keys.

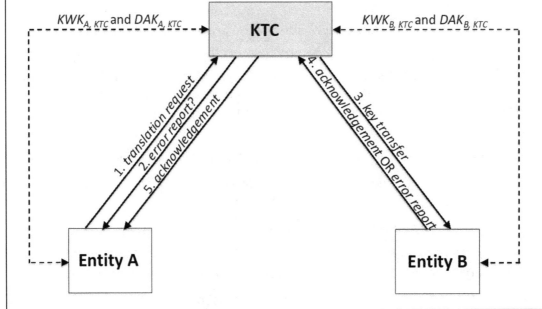

1902
1903   **Figure A.4: Using a KTC**

1. (a) Entity A generates a KWK ($KWK_{A, B}$) and an authentication key ($DAK_{A, B}$) to be sent to Entity B, and another authentication key (*Transaction_auth_key*) to provide authentication for the *translation request* to be sent to the KTC.

    (b) Entity A wraps the generated keys using the KWK shared with the KTC ($KWK_{A, KTC}$):

    $$wrapped\_keys = \text{WRAP}(KWK_{A, KTC}, KWK_{A, B} \| DAK_{A, B} \| Transaction\_auth\_key).$$

    Note that in this example, $KWK_{A, B}$ and $DAK_{A, B}$ are wrapped using the same key (i.e., $KWK_{A, KTC}$). In this case, $KWK_{A, B}$ and $DAK_{A, B}$ are both Layer 1 keys.

    (c) Entity A prepares and sends a message containing *translation request* information to the KTC with the wrapped keys:

    translation_request(*wrapped_keys*; *requester*: Entity_A; *sharing_entities*: Entity_A, Entity_B; *auth_code₁*),

    where *auth_code₁* is generated using the message's authentication key (*Transaction_auth_key*).

2. The KTC unwraps the wrapped keying material in the *translation request* information and uses the unwrapped message authentication key (*Transaction_auth_key*) to verify the message. If the verification fails, an error report is sent to Entity A:

    error_report(*previous_message_id*; *error_type*; *auth_code₂*),

    where *previous_message_id* is the ID for the message containing the *translation request* information (see step 1), the *error_type* is the type of error, and *auth_code₂* is generated using $DAK_{A, KTC}$. Note that since there was an error in the message, the wrapped authentication key (*Transaction_auth_key*) in the *translation request* information may not be correct, so $DAK_{A, KTC}$ is used as the authentication key.

    Entity A may choose to resend the *translation request* information (not shown in the figure).

3. (a) If the authentication code is successfully verified, the KTC wraps the received keys for Entity B using the KWK shared with B ($KWK_{B, KTC}$):

    $$wrapped\_keys = \text{WRAP}(KWK_{B, KTC}, KWK_{A, B} \| DAK_{A, B} \| Transaction\_auth\_key).$$

    (b) The KTC prepares and sends a message to Entity B containing the wrapped keys as *key transfer* information and generates *auth_code₃* on the message using the received authentication key (*Transaction_auth_key*):

    key_transfer(*wrapped_keys*; *communicating_group*: Entity_A, Entity_B; *auth_code₃*).

4. (a) Entity B unwraps the received keys and attempts to verify *auth_code₃* using the authentication key included in the message containing the *key transfer* information (*Transaction_auth_key*); see step 3b.

    (b) If the verification fails or if Entity B does not want to establish a communicating group with Entity A, a message containing *error report* information is returned to the KTC, and the process is terminated.

    error_report(*previous_message_id*; *error_type*; *auth_code₄*), where *previous_message_id* is the ID for the message containing the *key transfer* information (see step 3b), *error_type* is the type of error, and *auth_code$_4$* is generated on the error message using $DAK_{B,\ KTC}$. Note that when there is an error in the received message, the wrapped authentication key (*Transaction_auth_key*) in the *key transfer* information may not be correct, so $DAK_{B,\ KTC}$ is used as the authentication key. Also, if Entity B does not want to establish a communicating group with Entity A, using the authentication key received in the *key transfer* information (*Transaction_auth_key*) may not be desirable.

The KTC may choose to resend the *key transfer* information (not shown in the figure).

(c) If the verification is successful, and Entity B wants to establish a communicating with Entity A, Entity B sends a message containing *acknowledgement* information to the KTC:

$$\textbf{\textit{acknowledgement}}(\textit{previous\_msg\_id};\ \textit{auth\_code}_5),$$

where *previous_message_id* is the ID for the message containing the *key-transfer* information (see step 3b), and *auth_code$_5$* is generated on the message using *Transaction_auth_key*.

5. If the message containing the *acknowledgement* information is received correctly from Entity B[43], then the KTC prepares and sends a message containing *acknowledgement* information to Entity A indicating that the communicating group has been established successfully:

$$\textbf{\textit{acknowledgement}}(\textit{previous\_msg\_id};\ \textit{auth\_code}_6),$$

where *previous_message_id* is the ID for the message containing the *translation request* information (see step 1b), and *auth_code$_6$* is generated using *Transaction_auth_key*.

Note that for the sake of brevity, Entity A's receipt and handling of the *acknowledgement* information is not discussed in detail here. However, if the message containing the *acknowledgement* information cannot be verified, then Entity A could send an error message to the KTC, and the KTC could resend the *acknowledgement* information above.

Note: alternatively, a special-purpose confirmation message could be used to indicate successful communicating-group establishment.

A.5   Using a Multiple-Center Group to Generate a Key for Establishing a Communicating Group

A communicating group may be established using the services of a multiple-center group to generate the Layer 1 keys to be shared by the members of a communicating group. In this example (shown as Figure A.5), the multiple-center group consists of Center 1 and Center 2; these centers share a KWK and a DAK (e.g., $KWK_{1,2}$ and $DAK_{1,2}$). Center 1 is Entity A's agent to the group; they share $KWK_{A,1}$ and $DAK_{A,1}$. Center 2 is Entity B's agent to the group; they share $KWK_{B,2}$ and $DAK_{B,2}$. Entities A and B do not currently share keys.

In this example, Center 1 generates keying material at Entity A's request and sends it to Center 2 for translation for Entity B. Center 2 translates the keying material for Entity B and sends it to B. After receiving an acknowledgement that the keys have been received correctly by Entity B, Center

---

[43] The handling of errors in the received acknowledgement is left to the reader.

1979 2 sends an acknowledgement of correct receipt to Center 1, who forwards the acknowledgement
1980 to Entity A; the communicating group is then considered to be established.

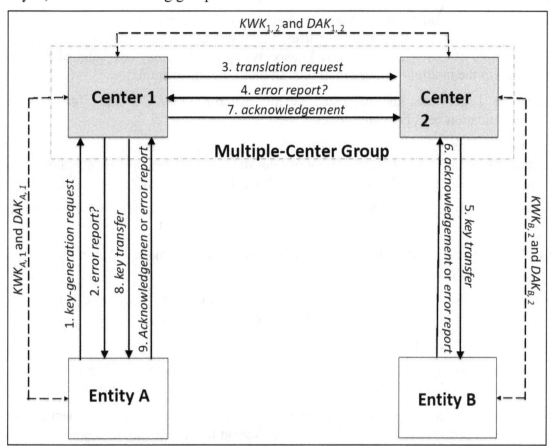

1981
1982 **Figure A.5: Establishing a Communicating Group Using a Multiple-Center Group for Key**
1983 **Generation**

1984 1. Entity A may optionally send a *key-generation request* to its agent asking for the generation of
1985   a KWK and DAK to be used with Entity B.

1986   ***key-generation_request***(KWK, DAK; *communicating_group*: Entity_A, Entity_B;
1987   *auth_code$_1$*).

1988 where *auth_code$_1$* is generated on the message containing the *key_generation request*
1989 information using $DAK_{A,1}$.

1990 2. Center 1 attempts to verify *auth_code$_1$* using the DAK shared with Entity A (i.e., $DAK_{A,1}$). If
1991   the verification fails, an error message containing *error report* information is returned to Entity
1992   A, and the process is terminated.

1993   ***error_report***(*previous_message_id*; *error_type*; *auth_code$_2$*),

1994 where *previous_message_id* is the ID for the message containing the *key-generation request*
1995 information (see step 1), the *error_type* is the type of error, and *auth_code$_2$* is generated
1996 using $DAK_{A,1}$.

1997 Entity A may choose to resend the *key-generation request* information (not shown in the
1998 figure).

1999 3. (a) If the verification of the message containing the key-*generation request* information is
2000 successful, but the other entity identified in the *key-generation request* (Entity B) is not a
2001 subscriber of Center 1, then Center 1 suspects that Entity B may be a subscriber of another
2002 center in the multiple-center group (i.e., Center 2 in this example).

2003 (b) Center 1 generates the requested keying material ($KWK_{A, B}$ and $DAK_{A, B}$) and an
2004 authentication key (*Transaction_auth_key*).

2005 (c) Center 1 needs to send *translation request* information to Center 2, so another
2006 authentication key is generated (*Group_Transaction_auth_key*) and wrapped with the keys
2007 to be translated using the KWK shared with Center 2 ($KWK_{1,2}$).

2008 $Center\_2\_wrapped\_keys = WRAP(KWK_{1, 2}, KWK_{A, B} \parallel DAK_{A, B} \parallel Transaction\_auth\_key \parallel$
2009 $Group\_Transaction\_auth\_key)$.

2010 (d) Center 1 prepares and sends a message to Center 2 containing *translation request*
2011 information with the wrapped keys:

2012 **translation_request**(*Center_2_wrapped_keys*; *requester*: Center_1; *communicating_group*:
2013 Entity_A, Entity B; *auth_code₃*),

2014 where *auth_code₃* is generated using *Group_Transaction_auth_key*.

2015 4. (a) Center 2 unwraps the keys in the *translation request* information using $KWK_{1,2}$ to obtain
2016 the authentication key used for the message (*Group_Transaction_auth_key*).

2017 (b) Center 2 attempts to verify *auth_code₃* using the unwrapped authentication key
2018 (*Group_Transaction_auth_key*). If the verification fails, or Entity B is not a subscriber of
2019 Center 2, a message containing *error report* information is returned to Center 1, and the
2020 process is terminated.

2021 **error_report**(*previous_message_id*; *error_type*; *auth_code₄*),

2022 where *previous_message_id* is the ID for the message containing the *translation request*
2023 information (see step 3d), the *error_type* is the type of error, and *auth_code₄* is generated
2024 using $DAK_{1, 2}$. Note that since there was an error in the received message, the wrapped
2025 authentication key (*Group_Transaction_auth_key*) in the received message may not be
2026 correct, so $DAK_{1, 2}$ is used as the authentication key.

2027 Center 1 may choose to resend the *translation request* information (not shown in the
2028 figure).

2029 Center 1 may notify Entity A of the problem in an error message (not shown in the figure).

2030 5. (a) If the verification was successful and Entity B is a subscriber of Center 2, Center 2
2031 translates the keying material by wrapping it in the KWK shared with Entity B ($KWK_{B, 2}$):

2032 $Entity\_B\ wrapped\_keys = WRAP(KWK_{B, 2}, KWK_{A, B}, DAK_{A, B} \parallel Transaction\_auth\_key)$.

2033 (b) Center 2 then prepares and sends a message containing the *key transfer* information to
2034 Entity B.

2035
2036

key_transfer(*Entity_B_wrapped_keys*; *communicating_group: Entity_A, Entity_B;*
auth_code$_5$),

2037

where *auth_code*$_5$ is generated using *Transaction_auth_key*.

2038
2039
2040
2041
2042

6. (a) Entity B unwraps the received keying material and attempts to verify *auth_code*$_5$ using the transaction authentication key provided in the *key transfer* information (*Transaction_auth_key*). If the verification fails, or Entity B does not wish to establish a communicating group with Entity A, a message containing *error report* information is returned to Center 2:

2043

error_report(*previous_message_id*; *error_type*; *auth_code*$_6$),

2044
2045
2046
2047
2048
2049
2050

where *previous_message_id* is the ID for the message containing the *key transfer* information (see step 5b), the *error_type* is the type of error, and *auth_code*$_6$ is generated using $DAK_{B,2}$. Note that when there is an error in the received message, the wrapped authentication key (*Transaction_auth_key*) in the *key transfer* information may not be correct, so $DAK_{B,2}$ is used as the authentication key. Also, if Entity B does not want to establish a communicating group with Entity A, using the authentication key received in the *key transfer* information (*Transaction_auth_key*) may not be desirable.

2051
2052

Center 2 may choose to resend the *key transfer* information if the previous message was in error (not shown in the figure).

2053
2054
2055

(b) If the verification is successful, and Entity B wishes to establish a communicating group with Entity A, Entity B sends a message containing *acknowledgement* information to Center 2:

2056

acknowledgement(*previous_msg_id*; *auth_code*$_7$),

2057
2058

where *previous_message_id* is the ID for the message containing the *key-transfer* information (see step 5b), and *auth_code*$_7$ is generated using *Transaction_auth_key*.

2059
2060
2061

7. If the acknowledgement is received correctly from Entity B, then the Center 2 forwards the *acknowledgement* information to Center 1, indicating that the communicating group has been established successfully:

2062

acknowledgement(*previous_msg_id*; *auth_code*$_8$),

2063
2064

where *previous_message_id* is the ID for the message containing the *translation request* information (see step 3d), and *auth_code*$_8$ is generated using *Group_Transaction_auth_key*.

2065
2066
2067
2068

For the sake of brevity, Center 1's receipt and verification of the message received from Center 2 containing the *acknowledgement* information is not discussed in detail here. However, if there is an error in the message, Center 1 could send a message to Center 2 containing *error report* information, and Center 2 could resend the *acknowledgement* information above.

2069
2070
2071

8. (a) Assuming that the message containing the *acknowledgement* information is received correctly from Center 2, Center 1 wraps the keys for Entity A using the KWK shared with Entity A (*KWK$_{A,1}$*):

2072

Entity_A_wrapped_keys = WRAP($KWK_{A,1}$, $KWK_{A,B}$ || $DAK_{A,B}$ || *Transaction_auth_key*).

2073   (b) Center 1 then prepares and sends a message containing the *key transfer* information to
2074   Entity A:

2075   **key_transfer**(*Entity_A_wrapped_keys*; *communicating_group*: Entity_A, Entity_B;
2076   *auth_code$_9$*),

2077   where *auth_code$_9$* is generated using *Transaction_auth_key*.

2078 9. (a) Entity A attempts to verify *auth_code$_9$* using the transaction authentication key provided
2079   in the *key transfer* information (*Transaction_auth_key*). If the verification fails, a message
2080   containing *error report* information is returned to Center 1:

2081   **error_report**(*previous_message_id*; *error_type*; *auth_code$_{10}$*),

2082   where *previous_message_id* is the ID for the message containing the *key transfer*
2083   information (see step 8b), the *error_type* is the type of error, and *auth_code$_6$* is generated
2084   using $DAK_{4,1}$. Note that when there is an error in the received message, the wrapped
2085   authentication key (*Transaction_auth_key*) in the *key transfer* information may not be
2086   correct, so $DAK_{4,1}$ is used as the authentication key.

2087   Center 1 may choose to resend the *key transfer* information if the previous message was in
2088   error (not shown in the figure).

2089   (b) If the message containing the *key transfer* information is received correctly from Center 1,
2090   then the Entity A sends the *acknowledgement* information to Center 1 indicating that the
2091   key transfer information was received correctly:

2092   **acknowledgement**(*previous_msg_id*; *auth_code$_{11}$*),

2093   where *previous_message_id* is the ID for the message containing the *key transfer*
2094   information (see step 8b), and *auth_code$_{11}$* is generated using *Transactiun_auth_key*.

2095   Note that for the sake of brevity, Center 1's receipt and handling of the *acknowledgement*
2096   information is not discussed in detail here. However, if the message containing the
2097   *acknowledgement* information cannot be verified, then Center 1 could send an error
2098   message to Entity A, and Entity A could resend the *acknowledgement* information above.

2099 At this point, Entities A and B share a KWK and DAK as members of the same communicating
2100 group. However, only Entity A knows for sure that the keys are shared (because of the order that
2101 the keys were distributed by the multiple-center group in this example). Entity B could be notified
2102 of this fact by Entity A or B sending a cryptographically protected message to the other party (e.g.,
2103 protected using the newly established KWK and DAK). Alternatively, a special purpose-
2104 confirmation message could be used to indicate successful establishment of the communicating
2105 group.

A.6   Using a Multiple-Center Group to Establish a Communicating Group Only Using its Key-Translation Services

2106
2107

2108 Figure A.6 depicts an example of information flow for establishing a communicating group using
2109 the key-translation services of a multiple-center group. In this example, Center 1 and Center 2 are
2110 members of the same multiple-center group and share a KWK
2111 ($KWK_{1,2}$) and an authentication key ($DAK_{1,2}$). Entity A's agent to the group is Center 1; they share

2112 $KWK_{A,1}$ and $DAK_{A,1}$. Entity B's agent to the group is Center 2; they share $KWK_{B,2}$ and $DAK_{B,2}$.
2113   Entity A and Center 1 can generate keys, but Center 2 cannot. Entities A and B wish to establish
2114   a communicating group.

2115   Note that this example is very similar to the example in Appendix A.5; the main difference is that
2116   Entity A can generate keys.

2117   In this example, Entity A generates keying material and sends it to its agent for translation for
2118   Entity B. Center 1 forwards the keying material to Center 2 for translation and providing the
2119   translated keying material to Entity B. After receiving an acknowledgement from Entity B that the
2120   keys have been received correctly, Center 2 sends an acknowledgement of correct receipt to Center
2121   1, who forwards the acknowledgement to Entity A; the communicating group is then considered
2122   to be established.

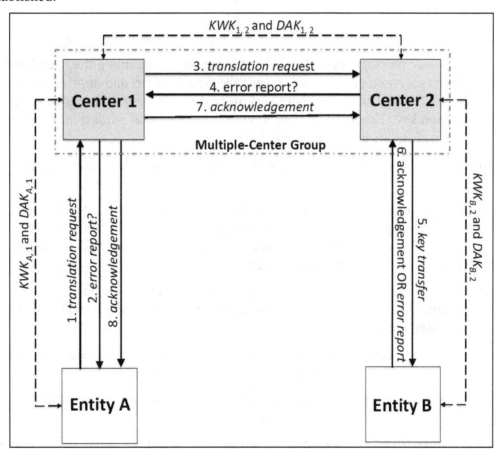

2123

2124   **Figure A.6: Using the Translation Services of a Multiple-Center Group to Establish a**
2125   **Communicating Group**

2126   1. (a) Entity A generates a KWK, a DAK and a transaction authentication key
2127   (*Transaction_auth_key*) to be sent to Entity B.

2128   (b) Entity A wraps the keys in the KWK shared with its agent ($KWK_{A,1}$):

2129   *wrapped_keys* = WRAP($KWK_{A,1}$, $KWK_{A,B}$ ‖ $DAK_{A,B}$ ‖ *Transaction_auth_key*).

2130 (c) Entity A prepares and sends a message containing *translation request* information to Center
2131 1 that includes the wrapped keys:

2132 ***translation_request***(*wrapped_keys*; *requester*: Entity_A; *communicating_group*:
2133 Entity_A, Entity B; *auth_code*$_1$),

2134 where *auth_code*$_1$ is generated using the generated authentication key
2135 (*Transaction_auth_key*).

2136 2. (a) Center 1 unwraps the wrapped keying material in the *translation request* information and
2137 uses the unwrapped transaction authentication key (*Transaction_auth_*key) to verify the
2138 message containing the *translation request* information.

2139 (b) If the verification fails, a message is sent to Entity A containing the *error report*
2140 information:

2141 ***error_report***(*previous_message_id*; *error_type; auth_code*$_2$),

2142 where *previous_message_id* is the ID for the message containing the *translation request*
2143 information (see step 1c), the *error_type* is the type of error, and *auth_code*$_2$ is computed
2144 using $DAK_{A,\,1}$. Note that since there was an error in the received message, the wrapped
2145 authentication key (*Transaction_auth_key*) in the *translation request* information may not
2146 be correct, so $DAK_{A,\,1}$ is used as the authentication key.

2147 Entity A may choose to resend the *translation request* information (not shown in the
2148 figure).

2149 3. If the verification of the message containing the *key-generation request* is successful, but the
2150 other entity identified in the *key-generation request* information (Entity B) is not a subscriber
2151 of Center 1, then Center 1 suspects that Entity B may be a subscriber of another center in the
2152 multiple-center group (i.e., Center 2 in this example).

2153 (a) Center 1 needs to send *translation request* information to Center 2, so generates an
2154 authentication key (*Group_Transaction_auth_key*) and wraps it with the keys to be
2155 translated using the KWK shared with Center 2 ($KWK_{1,2}$).

2156 *Center_2_wrapped_keys* = WRAP($KWK_{1,2}$, $KWK_{A,\,B}$ || $DAK_{A,\,B}$ || *Transaction_auth_key* ||
2157 *Group_Transaction_auth_key*).

2158 (b) Center 1 prepares and sends a message containing *translation request* information to
2159 Center 2 that includes the wrapped keys:

2160 **translation_request**(*Center_2_wrapped_keys*; *requester*: Center_1; *communicating_group*:
2161 Entity_A, Entity B; *auth_code*$_3$),

2162 where *auth_code*$_3$ is generated using *Group_Transaction_auth_key*.

2163 4. (a) Center 2 unwraps the *translation request* information to obtain the authentication key
2164 (*Group_Transaction_auth_key*).

2165 (b) Center 2 attempts to verify *auth_code*$_3$ using the unwrapped authentication key
2166 (*Group_Transaction_auth_key*). If the verification fails, or if Entity B is not a subscriber
2167 of Center 2, a message containing *error report* information is returned to Center 1, and the
2168 process is terminated.

2169   ***error_report***(*previous_message_id*; *error_type*; *auth_code$_4$*),

2170   where *previous_message_id* is the ID for the message containing the *translation request*
2171   information (see step 3b), the *error_type* is the type of error, and *auth_code$_4$* is computed
2172   on the message using $DAK_{1,2}$. Note that since there was an error in the received message,
2173   the wrapped authentication key (*Group_Transaction_auth_key*) in the *translation request*
2174   information may not be correct, so $DAK_{1,2}$ is used as the authentication key for the message
2175   containing the *error report* information.

2176   Center 1 may choose to resend the *translation request* information or to notify Entity A of
2177   the problem in an error message (not shown in the figure).

2178 5. (a) If the verification is successful, and Entity is a subscriber of Center 2, Center 2 translates
2179   the keys ($KWK_{A,B}$ $\|$ $DAK_{A,B}$ $\|$ *Transaction_auth_key*) by wrapping them in the KWK
2180   shared with Entity B *($KWK_{B,2}$)*:

2181   *Entity_B wrapped_key*s = WRAP($KWK_{B,2}$, $KWK_{A,B}$ $\|$ $DAK_{A,B}$ $\|$ *Transaction_auth_key*).

2182   (b) Center 2 then prepares and sends a message containing the *key transfer* information to
2183   Entity B.

2184   ***key_transfer***(*Entity_B_wrapped_keys*; *communicating_group*: Entity_A, Entity_B;
2185   *auth_code$_5$*),

2186   where *auth_code$_5$* is generated on the message using *Transaction_auth_key*.

2187 6. (a) Entity B unwraps the *key transfer* information and attempts to verify *auth_code$_5$* using the
2188   unwrapped authentication key (*Transaction_auth_key*).

2189   (b) If the verification fails, or Entity B does not want to establish a communicating group with
2190   Entity A, a message is sent to Center 2 containing *error report* inoformation.

2191   ***error_report***(*previous_message_id*; *error_type*; *auth_code$_6$*),

2192   where *previous_message_id* is the ID for the message containing the *key transfer*
2193   information (see step 5b), the *error_type* is the type of error, and *auth_code$_6$* is computed
2194   using $DAK_{B,2}$. Note that since there was an error in the received message, the wrapped
2195   authentication key (*Transaction_auth_key*) in the *key transfer* information may not be
2196   correct, so $DAK_{B,2}$ is used as the authentication key for the message containing the *error*
2197   *report* information.

2198   Center 2 may choose to resend the *key transfer* information (not shown in the figure) (see
2199   step 5b).

2200   Alternatively, Center 2 could send a message containing *error report* information to Center
2201   1 indicating that the keys could not be established between Entities A and B, authenticating
2202   the message using $DAK_{1,2}$; Center 1 could then forward the information to Entity A,
2203   authenticating the message using $DAK_{A,1}$. The transaction would then be considered as
2204   terminated. These messages are not shown in the figure.

2205   (c) If the verification is successful, and Entity B wants to establish a communicating group
2206   with Entity A, Entity B sends a message containing *acknowledgement* information to
2207   Center 2:

2208   ***acknowledgement***(*previous_msg_id*; *auth_code₇*),

2209   where *previous_message_id* is the ID for the message containing the *key transfer*
2210   information, and *auth_code₇* is generated using *Transaction_auth_key*.

2211 7. If a message containing *acknowledgement* information is received correctly from Entity B,
2212   then Center 2 sends a message containing *acknowledgement* information to Center 1, indicating
2213   that the communicating group has been established successfully:

2214   ***acknowledgement***(*previous_msg_id*; *auth_code₈*),

2215   where *previous_message_id* is the ID for the message containing the *translation request*
2216   information (see step 3b), and *auth_code₈* is generated using *Group_Transaction_auth_key*.

2217 8. If a message containing *acknowledgement* information is received correctly from Center 2,
2218   then Center 1 sends a message containing *acknowledgement* information to Entity A indicating
2219   that the communicating group has been established successfully:

2220   ***acknowledgement***(*previous_msg_id*; *auth_code₉*),

2221   where *previous_message_id* is the ID for the message containing the *key-generation request*
2222   information (see step 1c), and *auth_code₉* is generated using *Transaction_auth_key*.

2223 At this point, Entities A and B share a KWK and DAK as members of the same communicating
2224 group. However, only Entity A knows for sure that the keys are shared. Entity B could be notified
2225 of this fact by Entity A or B sending a cryptographically protected message to the other party (e.g.,
2226 protected using the newly established KWK and DAK). Alternatively, a special-purpose
2227 confirmation message could be used to indicate successful establishment of the communicating
2228 group.

A.7   Forwarding Keys Through an Intermediate Entity

2230 Keying material can be forwarded to the ultimate recipient(s) through intermediate entities (see
2231 Figure A.7 for an example). In this example, a KDC shares a KWK and DAK with Entity A, and
2232 Entity A shares KWKs and DAKs as the Layer 1 keys with Entities B and C, i.e.,

2233   • The KDC shares $KWK_{A,\,KDC}$ and $DAK_{A,\,KDC}$ with Entity A;

2234   • Entity A shares $KWK_{A,\,B}$ and $DAK_{A,\,B}$ with Entity B; and

2235   • Entity A shares $KWK_{A,\,C}$ and $DAK_{A,\,C}$ with Entity C.

2236 In this example, the KDC generates keying material (e.g., an AEK) to be shared by Entities B and
2237 C and distributes it via one of its subscribers (Entity A). Entities B and C become a communicating
2238 group, but since they do not share a KWK, they cannot generate further keys without the assistance
2239 of the KDC. Although Entity A is privy to the keys (since it assisted in their distribution), Entity
2240 A is not intended to be part of that communicating group for this example.

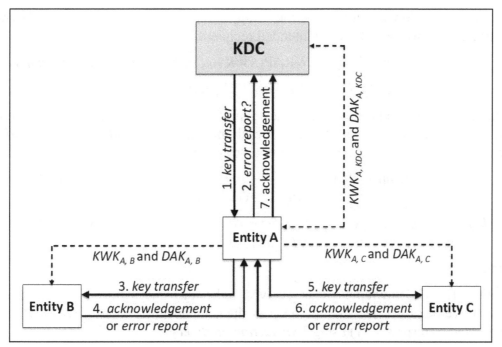

Figure A.7: *key transfer* through an Intermediate Entity

1. (a) The KDC generates an AEK and authentication keys (*Transaction_auth_key*$_1$ and *Transaction_auth_key*$_2$) to be used for message authentication and wraps them for Entity A.

wrapped_keys = WRAP(*KWK$_{A, KDC}$*, *AEK$_{B,C}$* ‖ *Transaction_auth_key*$_1$ ‖ *Transaction_auth_key*$_2$).

(b) The KDC prepares and sends a message containing *key transfer* information to Entity A:

key_transfer(*wrapped_keys*; *communicating_group*: Entity B, Entity C; *auth_code*$_1$),

where *auth_code*$_1$ is computed on the message containing the *key transfer* information using *Transaction_auth_key*$_2$.

2. Entity A unwraps the *key transfer* information using the KWK shared with the KDC (*KWK$_{A, KDC}$*) and attempts to verify the received message using *Transaction_auth_key*$_2$.

(a) If the verification fails, an error message is sent to the KDC containing *error report* information:

error_report(*previous_message_id*; *error_type*; *auth_code*$_2$),

where *previous_message_id* is the ID for the message containing the *key transfer* information (see step 1b), the *error_type* is the type of error, and *auth_code*$_2$ is generated using *DAK$_{A, KDC}$*. Note that since there was an error in the received message, the wrapped authentication key (*Transaction_auth_key*$_2$) in the message may not be correct, so *DAK$_{A, KDC}$* is used as the authentication key.

The KDC may choose to resend the *key transfer* information (not shown in the figure).

Steps 3 and 5 (these steps are combined to avoid repetitious descriptions):

70

2263 (a) If the verification is successful, the wrapped keys destined for Entities B and C are
2264 extracted and wrapped for each intended recipient:

2265 $Entity\_B\_wrapped\_keys = \text{WRAP}(KWK_{A,\,B}, AEK_{B,C} \parallel Transaction\_auth\_key_1)$.

2266 $Entity\_C\_wrapped\_keys = \text{WRAP}(KWK_{A,\,C}, AEK_{B,C} \parallel Transaction\_auth\_key_1)$.

2267 (b) The appropriate wrapped keys are placed in *key transfer* messages for each recipient, and
2268 an authentication code is computed for each message ($auth\_code_3$ and $auth\_code_4$) using
2269 the appropriate transaction authentication key (*Transaction_auth_key*$_1$):

2270 **key_transfer**(*Entity_B_wrapped_keys*; *communicating_group*: Entity_B, Entity_C;
2271 *auth_code*$_3$) is sent to Entity B.

2272 **key_transfer**(*Entity_C_wrapped_keys*; *communicating_group*: Entity_B, Entity_C;
2273 *auth_code*$_4$) is sent to Entity B.

2274 Steps 4 and 6:

2275 (a) Entities B and C unwrap the keys received in the *key transfer* information of their
2276 respective messages and attempt to verify the authentication codes (*auth_code*$_3$ and
2277 *auth_code*$_4$, respectively) using *Transaction_auth_key*$_1$.

2278 (b) If the verification fails, or the receiving entity does not want to be a member of the
2279 communicating group, a message is sent to Entity A containing *error report* information:

2280 Entity B would send **error_report**(*previous_message_id*; *error_type*; *auth_code*$_5$)

2281 Entity C would send **error_report**(*previous_message_id*; *error_type*; *auth_code*$_6$)

2282 where *previous_message_id* is the ID for the message containing the *key transfer*
2283 information (see step 3/5 b), and the *error_type* is the type of error. Entity B would
2284 generate *auth_code*$_5$ using $DAK_{A,\,B}$; Entity C would generate *auth_code*$_6$ using $DAK_{A,\,C}$.
2285 Note that since there was an error in the received message, the wrapped authentication
2286 key (*Transaction_auth_key*$_1$) in the *key transfer* information may not be correct, so $DAK_{A,\,B}$
2287 $_B$ and $DAK_{A,\,C}$ would be used as the authentication keys.

2288 Entity A may choose to resend the *key transfer* information (not shown in the figure).

2289 (c) If the verification is successful, and both entities want to establish a communicating
2290 group with each other, a message containing *acknowledgement* information is sent to
2291 Entity A:

2292 Entity B would send **acknowledgement**(*previous_msg_id*; *auth_code*$_7$)

2293 Entity C would send **acknowledgement**(*previous_msg_id*; *auth_code*$_8$),

2294 where *previous_message_id* is the ID for the message containing the *key transfer*
2295 information (see step 3/5 b), and *auth_code*$_7$ and *auth_code*$_8$ are generated using
2296 *Transaction_auth_key*$_1$.

2297 7. If the message containing the *acknowledgement* information is received correctly from both
2298 Entities B and C, then Entity A sends a message to the KDC containing *acknowledgement*
2299 information indicating that the communicating group has been established successfully:

2300 $$acknowledgement(previous\_msg\_id; auth\_code_9),$$

2301 where *previous_message_id* is the ID for the message containing the *key-transfer* information
2302 (see step 1b), and *auth_code$_9$* is generated using *Transaction_auth_key$_2$*.

2303 At this point, Entities B and C share an AEK as members of the same communicating group.
2304 However, only Entity A and the KDC know for sure that the keys are shared. Enitites B and C
2305 could be notified of this fact in a couple of ways:

2306 • By Entity B or C sending a cryptographically protected message to the other party (e.g.,
2307 protected using the newly established AEK); or

2308 • By Entity A sending *acknowledgement* information to Entities B and C indicating that the
2309 establishment of the communicating group has been completed (not shown in the figure).

A.8 Requesting Key Revocation and Confirmation

2310

A.8.1 Example 1

2311

2312 Figure A.8a is an example of using a *revocation request* and corresponding *revocation
2313 confirmation*. In this example, a KDC sends a revocation request to the members of a
2314 communicating group (Entities A and B) to terminate the group by revoking the Level 1 key in
2315 their key hierarchy ($KWK_{A, B}$); presumably, the KDC was a participant in establishing that key.
2316 Entity A shares $KWK_{A, KDC}$ and $DAK_{A, KDC}$ with the KDC; Entity B shares $KWK_{B, KDC}$ and $DAK_{B, KDC}$ with the KDC.
2317 $_{KDC}$ with the KDC.

2318 The keys shared by Entities A and B consist of a Layer 1 key ($KWK_{A,B}$) and a layer 2 $DAK_{A, B}$,
2319 which were established previously using the KDC (see Appendix A.3), and several lower-layer
2320 keys established within the communicating group (i.e., Entities A and B) using $KWK_{A, B}$ after the
2321 group was established (see Appendix A.1 for the process):

2322 • $KWK_{A, B}$ was used to wrap KWK_{Layer_2} and DAK_{Layer_2}.

2323 • KWK_{Layer_2} was used to wrap KDK_{Layer_3}, and

2324 • KDK_{Layer_3} was used to derive DEK_{Layer_4} and DAK_{Layer_4}.

2325 In this example, the revocation request is sent directly to each entity by the KDC so that each will
2326 acknowledge that they have fulfilled the request. Note that in this example, both revocation
2327 requests are sent before expecting the return of the corresponding *revocation confirmation* or *error
2328 report* information. This is a design decision for this example (not a requirement) to allow each
2329 entity to find and destroy all copies of keys affected by the *revocation request* information (i.e.,
2330 all keys lower in the key hierarchy).

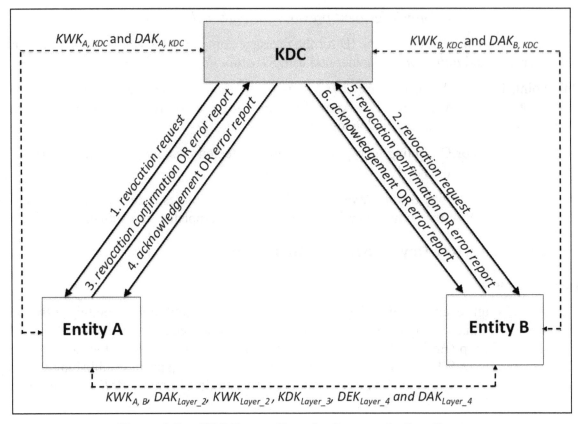

2331

Figure A.8a: KDC Revocation of a Communicating Group

2333 1. (a) The KDC generates an authentication key (*Transaction_auth_key$_A$*) for the message
2334   containing the *revocation request* information to be sent to Entity A and wraps it using the
2335   KWK shared with Entity A (*KWK$_{A,\ KDC}$*):

2336   *wrapped_auth_key_A* = WRAP(*KWK$_{A,\ KDC}$*, *Transaction_auth_key$_A$*).

2337   (b) The KDC prepares and sends a message to Entity A containing *revocation request*
2338   information that requests that Entity A revoke the Level 1 KWK (*KWK$_{A,\ B}$*) shared with
2339   Entity B and all keys beneath it in the key hierarchy:

2340   **revocation_request**(ID of *KWK$_{A,\ B}$*; *wrapped_auth_key_A*; *auth_code$_1$*),

2341   where *auth_code$_1$* is generated on the message using *Transaction_auth_key$_A$*.

2342 2. (a) Likewise, the KDC generates an authentication key (*Transaction_auth_key$_B$*) for the
2343   message containing the *revocation request* information to be sent to Entity B and wraps it
2344   using the KWK shared with Entity B (*KWK$_{B,\ KDC}$*):

2345   *wrapped_auth_key_B* = WRAP(*KWK$_{B,\ KDC}$*, *Transaction_auth_key$_B$*).

2346   (b) The KDC prepares and sends a message to Entity B containing the *revocation request*
2347   information that requests that Entity B revoke the Level 1 KWK (*KWK$_{A,\ B}$*) shared with
2348   Entity A:

2349   **revocation_request**(ID_of_*KWK$_{A,\ B}$*; *wrapped_auth_key_B*; *auth_code$_2$*),

2350   where *auth_code$_2$* is generated on the message using *Transaction_auth_key$_B$*.

2351 3. (a) Entity A unwraps the authentication key and attempts to verify the received message. If
2352   the verification fails, a message containing *error report* information is sent to the KDC and
2353   the process is terminated:

2354   **error_report**(*previous_message_id*; *error_type*; *auth_code$_3$*),

2355   where *previous_message_id* is the ID for the message containing the *revocation request*
2356   information (see step 1b), the *error_type* is the type of error, and *auth_code$_3$* is computed
2357   using *DAK$_{A, KDC}$*. Note that since there was an error in the received message, the wrapped
2358   authentication key (*Transaction_auth_key$_A$*) in the message may not be correct, so *DAK$_{A, KDC}$*
2359   is used as the authentication key.

2360   The KDC would most likely resend the message, in this case.

2361 (b) If the verification is successful, Entity A destroys all copies of *KWK$_{A, B}$* and any keys lower
2362   in the key hierarchy (i.e., *KWK$_{Layer\_2}$*, *DAK$_{Layer\_2}$*, *KDK$_{Layer\_3}$*, *DEK$_{Layer\_4}$* and *DAK$_{Layer\_4}$*).

2363 (c) Entity A prepares and sends a message containing *revocation confirmation* information to
2364   the KDC:

2365   **revocation_confirmation**(ID_of_*KWK$_{A, B}$*; *auth_code$_4$*),

2366   where *auth_code$_4$* is computed on the message using *Transaction_auth_key$_A$*.

2367 4. The KDC attempts to verify *auth_code$_4$* using the authentication key used for the message
2368 containing the *revocation request* information (see step 1b) (i.e., *Transaction_auth_key$_A$*).

2369 (a) If the verification fails, a message containing *error report* information is returned to Entity
2370   A, and the process is terminated.

2371   **error_report**(*previous_message_id*; *error_type*; *auth_code$_5$*),

2372   where *previous_message_id* is the ID for the message containing the *revocation*
2373   *confirmation* information (see step 3c), the *error_type* is the type of error, and *auth_code$_5$*
2374   is computed on the message using *Transaction_auth_key$_A$*. Since the *revocation request*
2375   was received correctly, *Transaction_auth_key$_A$* can be used.

2376   Entity A may choose to resend the message (not shown in the figure).

2377 (b) If the verification is successful, the KDC sends a message containing *acknowledgement*
2378   information to Entity A:

2379   **acknowledgement**(*previous_msg_id*; *auth_code$_6$*),

2380   where *previous_message_id* is the ID for the message containing the *revocation*
2381   *confirmation* information (see step 3c), and *auth_code$_6$* is generated on the message using
2382   *Transaction_auth_key$_A$*.

2383 5. (a) Entity B unwraps the authentication key and attempts to verify the received message. If the
2384   verification fails, a message containing *error report* information is sent to the KDC and
2385   the process is terminated:

2386   **error_report**(*previous_message_id*; *error_type*; *auth_code$_7$*), where *previous_message_id* is the ID for the message containing the *revocation request* information (see step 2b), the *error_type* is the type of error, and *auth_code$_7$* is computed on the message using $DAK_{B, KDC}$. Note that since there was an error in the received message, the wrapped authentication key (*Transaction_auth_key$_B$*) in the message may not be correct, so $DAK_{B, KDC}$ is used as the authentication key.

The KDC would most likely resend the message, in this case.

(b) If the verification is successful, Entity B destroys all copies of $KWK_{A, B}$ and any keys lower in the key hierarchy (i.e., KWK_{Layer_2}, DAK_{Layer_2}, KDK_{Layer_3}, DEK_{Layer_4} and DAK_{Layer_4}).

(c) Entity B prepares and sends a message containing *revocation confirmation* information to the KDC:

$$\textbf{\textit{revocation\_confirmation}}(ID\_of\_KWK_{A, B}; auth\_code_8),$$

where *auth_code$_8$* is computed on the message using *Transaction_auth_key$_B$*.

6. The KDC attempts to verify *auth_code$_8$* using the authentication key used for the message containing the *revocation request* information (see step 2b) (i.e., *Transaction_auth_key$_B$*).

(a) If the verification fails, a message containing the *error report* information is returned to Entity B, and the process is terminated.

$$\textbf{\textit{error\_report}}(previous\_message\_id; error\_type; auth\_code_9),$$

where *previous_message_id* is the ID for the message containing the *revocation confirmation* information (see step 5c), the *error_type* is the type of error, and *auth_code$_9$* is computed on the message using *Transaction_auth_key$_B$*. Since the *revocation request* was received correctly, *Transaction_auth_key$_B$* can be used.

Entity B may choose to resend the message (not shown in the figure).

(b) If the verification is successful, the KDC sends a message containing *acknowledgement* information to Entity B:

$$\textbf{\textit{acknowledgement}}(previous\_msg\_id; auth\_code_{10}),$$

where *previous_message_id* is the ID for the message containing the *revocation confirmation* information (see step 5c), and *auth_code$_{10}$* is generated on the message using *Transaction_auth_key$_B$*.

A.8.2 Example 2

In this example, a communicating group consists of Entities A and B, with shared keys shown in Figure A.8b. Entity A wishes to revoke the KDK and all keys below it in the key hierarchy (e.g., because the KDK has been compromised or has been used too many times to derive keys).

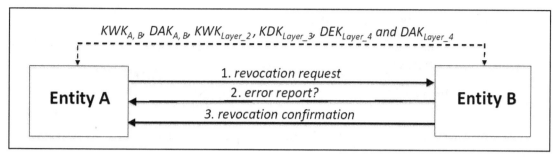

Figure A.8b: Revocation of Lower-level Keys

1. (a) If Entity A has a key-generation capability:

   - Entity A generates an authentication key (*Transaction_auth_key*) for the message containing the *revocation request* information to be sent to Entity B and wraps it using the KWK shared with Entity B ($KWK_{A, B}$):

     $$wrapped\_auth\_key = \text{WRAP}(KWK_{A, B}, Transaction\_auth\_key).$$

   - Entity A prepares and sends a message to Entity B containing *revocation request* information that requests that Entity B revoke the KDK shared with Entity A and all keys beneath it in the key hierarchy:

     revocation_request(ID_of_KDK_{Layer_3}; *wrapped_auth_key*; *auth_code$_1$*),

     where *auth_code$_1$* is generated on the message using *Transaction_auth_key*.

   (b) If Entity A does not have a key-generation capability:

   - Entity A will use $DAK_{A, B}$ as the authentication key for the message containing the *revocation request* information. Let "DAKAB" be the name of that key.

   - Entity A prepares and sends a message to Entity B containing *revocation request* information that requests that Entity B revoke the KDK shared with Entity A and all keys beneath it in the key hierarchy:

     revocation_request(ID_of_KDK_{Layer_3}; DAKAB ; *auth_code$_2$*),

     where *auth_code$_2$* is generated on the message using $DAK_{A, B}$.

2. (a) If a wrapped key is included in the *revocation request* information: Entity B unwraps the authentication key using $KWK_{A, B}$, obtaining *Transaction_auth_key*.

   (b) If the ID of an authentication key is included in the revocation request information, that key is used as the authentication key (i.e., $DAK_{A, B}$, in this case).

   (c) Entity B attempts to verify the received message. If the verification fails, a message containing *error report* information is sent to Entity A, and the process is terminated:

     error_report(*previous_message_id*; *error_type; auth_code$_3$*),

     where *previous_message_id* is the ID for the message containing the *revocation request* information (see step 1), the *error_type* is the type of error, and *auth_code$_3$* is computed using $DAK_{A, B}$. Note that since there was an error in the received message, $DAK_{A, B}$ is used as the authentication key.

2450   Entity A would most likely resend the message, in this case.

2451   3.   (a) If the verification is successful, Entity B destroys all copies of KDK_{Layer_3} and any keys
2452   lower in the key hierarchy (i.e., DEK_{Layer_4} and DAK_{Layer_4}).

2453   (b) Entity B prepares and sends a message containing *revocation confirmation* information to
2454   Entity A:

2455   ***revocation_confirmation***(ID_of_ KDK_{Layer_3}; *auth_code*$_4$),

2456   where *auth_code*$_4$ is computed on the message using the authenication key usd for the
2457   message containing the *revocation request* information (i.e., either *Transaction_auth_key*
2458   or $DAK_{A,\ B}$).

Appendix B: References

[DSKPP]   *Dynamic Symmetric Key Provisioning Protocol (DSKPP)*; RFC 6063; Doherty, Pei, Machani, and Nystrom; Internet Engineering Task Force, December 2010.

https://tools.ietf.org/html/rfc6063

[FIPS140-2]   *Security Requirements for Cryptographic Modules*, Federal Information Processing Standards (FIPS) Publication FIPS 140-2, U.S. Department of Commerce/NIST, December 3, 2002.

https://doi.org/10.6028/NIST.FIPS.140-2

[FIPS 180-4]   *The Secure Hash Standard*, Federal Information Processing Standards (FIPS) Publication FIPS-180-4, U. S. Department of Commerce/NIST, August 4, 2015.

https://doi.org/10.6028/NIST.FIPS.186-4

[FIPS-197]   *Advanced Encryption Standard (AES)*, Federal Information Processing Standards (FIPS) Publication FIPS 197, U. S. Department of Commerce/NIST, November 26, 2001.

https://doi.org/10.6028/NIST.FIPS.197

[FIPS 198-1]   *The Keyed-Hash Message Authentication Code (HMAC)*, Federal Information Processing Standards (FIPS) Publication FIPS 198-1, U. S. Department of Commerce/NIST, July 2008.

https://doi.org/10.6028/NIST.FIPS.198-1

[FIPS 199]   *Standards for Security Categorization of Federal Information and Information Systems*, Federal Information Processing Standards (FIPS) Publication FIPS 199, U. S. Department of Commerce/NIST, March 2006.

https://doi.org/10.6028/NIST.FIPS.199

[FIPS 200]   *Minimum Security Requirements for Federal Information and Information Systems*, , Federal Information Processing Standards (FIPS) Publication FIPS 200, U. S. Department of Commerce/NIST, February 2004.

https://doi.org/10.6028/NIST.FIPS.200

[FIPS 202]   *SHA-3 Standard: Permutation-Based Hash and Extendable-Output Functions*, Federal Information Processing Standards (FIPS) Publication FIPS-202, U. S. Department of Commerce/NIST, August 4, 2015.

https://doi.org/10.6028/NIST.FIPS.202

[Kerberos]   *Kerberos: The Network Authentication Protocol*, Massachusetts Institute of Technology, September 25, 2017

https://web.mit.edu/kerberos/

2494 2495 2496	[KM in WSN]	"Key Management in Wireless Sensor Networks;" Mansour, Chalhoub, and Lafourcade; *Journal of Sensor and Actuator Networks*, ISSN 2224-2708; September 7, 2015.
2497		http://www.mdpi.com/2224-2708/4/3/251
2498 2499 2500	[NISTIR 8105]	*Report on Post-Quantum Cryptography*; Chen, Jordan, Liu, Moody, Peralta, Perlner, and Smith-Tone; National Institute of Standards and Technology, April 2016.
2501		https://doi.org/10.6028/NIST.IR.8105
2502 2503	[NISTIR 8114]	*Report on Lightweight Cryptography*; NISTIR 8114; McKay, Bassham, Turan, and Mouha; National Institute of Standards and Technology, March 2017.
2504		https://doi.org/10.6028/NIST.IR.8114
2505 2506	[RFC 4107]	*Guidelines for Cryptographic Key Management*, RFC 4107, Bellovin and Housley, The Internet Society, June 2005.
2507		https://tools.ietf.org/html/rfc4107
2508 2509 2510	[S/MIME]	*Secure/Multipurpose Internet Mail Extensions (S/MIME) Version 3.2 Message Specification*, RFC 5751, Ramsdell and Turner, The Internet Society, January 2010.
2511		https://tools.ietf.org/html/rfc5751
2512 2513 2514		The IETF LAMPS working group (see https://tools.ietf.org/wg/lamps/) has been developing a replacement for RFC 5751; the latest draft is available at https://tools.ietf.org/wg/lamps/draft-ietf-lamps-rfc5751-bis/.
2515 2516 2517	[SP 800-38A]	*Recommendation for Block Cipher Modes of Operation: Methods and Techniques*, SP 800-38A, M. Dworkin, National Institute of Standards and Technology, December 2001.
2518		https://doi.org/10.6028/NIST.SP.800-38A
2519 2520 2521	[SP800-38B]	*Recommendation for Block Cipher Modes of Operation: the CMAC Authentication Mode for Authentication*, SP 800-38B, M. Dworkin, National Institute of Standards and Technology, October, 2016.
2522		https://doi.org/10.6028/NIST.SP.800-38B
2523 2524 2525	[SP 800-38C]	*Recommendation for Block Cipher Modes of Operation: the CCM Mode for Authentication and Confidentiality*, SP 800-38C, M. Dworkin, National Institute of Standards and Technology, May 2004.
2526		https://doi.org/10.6028/NIST.SP.800-38C
2527 2528 2529	[SP 800-38D]	*Recommendation for Block Cipher Modes of Operation: Galois/Counter Mode (GCM) and GMAC*, SP 800-38D, M. Dworkin, National Institute of Standards and Technology, November 2007.
2530		https://doi.org/10.6028/NIST.SP.800-38D

2531 2532 2533	[SP800-38E]	*Recommendation for Block Cipher Modes of Operation: the XTS-AES Mode for Confidentiality on Storage Devices*, SP 800-38E, M. Dworkin, January 2010.
2534		https://doi.org/10.6028/NIST.SP.800-38E
2535 2536 2537	[SP 800-38F]	*Recommendation for Block Cipher Modes of Operation: Methods for Key Wrapping*, SP 800-38F, M. Dworkin, National Institute of Standards and Technology, December 2012.
2538		https://doi.org/10.6028/NIST.SP.800-38F
2539 2540 2541	[SP 800-38G]	*Recommendation for Block Cipher Modes of Operation: Methods for Format-Preserving Encryption*, M. Dworkin, National Institute of Standards and Technology, March 2016.
2542		https://doi.org/10.6028/NIST.SP.800-38G
2543 2544 2545	[SP 800-56A]	*Recommendation for Pair-Wise Key Establishment Schemes Using Discrete Logarithm Cryptography*; SP 800-56A, Revision 2; E. Barker, L. Chen, A. Roginsky, and M. Smid; May 2010.
2546		https://doi.org/10.6028/NIST.SP.800-56Ar3
2547 2548 2549	[SP 800-56B]	*Recommendation for Pair-Wise Key Establishment Schemes Using Integer Factorization Cryptography*; SP 800-56B, Revision 1; E. Barker, L. Chen, and D. Moody; September 2014.
2550		https://doi.org/10.6028/NIST.SP.800-56Br1
2551 2552 2553	[SP800-57 Pt. 1]	*Recommendation for Key Management: Part 1: General*, Special Publication 800-57 Part 1, Revision 4, E. Barker, National Institute of Standards and Technology, January 2016.
2554		https://doi.org/10.6028/NIST.SP.800-57pt1r4
2555 2556 2557 2558	[SP 800-57 Pt. 2]	*Recommendation for Key Management: Part 2: Best Practices for Key Management Organizations*; Special Publication 800-57 Part 2, Revision 1 DRAFT, E. Barker, and W. Barker; National Institute of Standards and Technology; April 2018.
2559 2560		https://csrc.nist.gov/CSRC/media/Publications/sp/800-57-part-2/rev-1/draft/documents/sp800-57pt2-r1-draft.pdf
2561 2562 2563	[SP 800-57 Pt. 3]	*Recommendation for Key Management: Part 3: Application-Specific Key Management Guidance*, Special Publication 800-57 Part 3, E. Barker and Dang, National Institute of Standards and Technology January 2015.
2564		https://doi.org/10.6028/NIST.SP.800-57pt3r1
2565 2566 2567	[SP 800-88]	*Guidelines for Media Sanitization*; Special Publication 800-88; R. Kissel, M. Scholl, S. Skolochenko, and X. Li;_National Institute of Standards and Technology; September 2006.
2568		https://doi.org/10.6028/NIST.SP.800-88r1

2569 [SP 800-90A]   *Recommendation for Random Number Generation Using Deterministic*
2570   *Random Bit Generators*, SP 800-90A, Revision 1, E. Barker and J. Kelsey,
2571   National Institute of Standards and Technology; June 2015.

2572   https://doi.org/10.6028/NIST.SP.800-90Ar1

2573 [SP 800-108]   *Recommendation for Key Derivation Using Pseudorandom Functions*
2574   *(Revised)*, Special Publication 800-108, L. Chen, National Institute of
2575   Standards and Technology, October 2009.

2576   https://doi.org/10.6028/NIST.SP.800-108

2577 [SP 800-131A]   *Transitions: Recommendation for the Use of Cryptographic Algorithms and*
2578   *Key Lengths*, NIST SP 800-131A, Revision 1, E. Barker and Q. Dang,
2579   November 2015.

2580   https://doi.org/10.6028/NIST.SP.800-131Ar1

2581 [SP 800-152]   *A Profile for U.S. Federal Cryptographic Key Management Systems (CKMS)*;
2582   NIST SP 800-152; E. Barker, Smid, and Branstad; National Institute of
2583   Standards and Technology; October 2015

2584   https://doi.org/10.6028/NIST.SP.800-152

2585 [SP 800-175B]   Guideline for Using Cryptographic Standards in the Federal Government:
2586   Cryptographic Mechanisms, E. Barker, National Institute of Standards and
2587   Technology, August 2016.

2588   https://doi.org/10.6028/NIST.SP.800-175B

2589 [SP 800-185]   *SHA-3 Derived Functions: cSHAKE, KMAC, TupleHash, and ParallelHash*;
2590   NIST SP 800-185; Kelsey, Chang, and Perlner; National Institute of Standards
2591   and Technology; December 2016.

2592   https://doi.org/10.6028/NIST.SP.800-185

2593 [X9.17]   American National Standard X9.17, Financial Institution Key Management
2594   (Wholesale), April 1985, Withdrawn.

2595 [X9.28]   American National Standard X9.28, Financial Institution Multiple Center Key
2596   Management (Wholesale), June 1991, Withdrawn.